TOWARDS A NEW LANDSCAPE

Towards a new landscape

Nicholas Alfrey

Paul Barker

Margaret Drabble

Norbert Lynton

Richard Mabey

David Matthews

Kathleen Raine

William Vaughan

BERNARD JACOBSON LIMITED

Published in 1993 by Bernard Jacobson Limited
14A Clifford Street, London W1X 1RF

© Bernard Jacobson Limited and the authors 1993

ISBN 1 872784 12 7

Cover illustration
John Constable, *The Valley of the Stour (Dedham from Gun Hill)*,
1805–09, oil on paper laid down on canvas, 19½ × 23¾ in. (detail).
Board of Trustees of the Victoria and Albert Museum

Text illustrations
Page 8: Gravetye Manor. Wildlife Matters, Sussex
Page 16: Ben Nicholson, *Tuscany*, 1951, oil on board, 12 × 14 in.
    Bernard Jacobson Gallery
Page 24: photograph of Salle Church, Norfolk by Derek A. Edwards.
    Norfolk Museums Service
Page 32: Bill Brandt, *Willy Lott's Cottage*, 1975. Bernard Jacobson
    Gallery
Page 40: William Tillyer, *Horcum*, 1993, acrylic on canvas with relief
    panel, 36 × 42 in. Bernard Jacobson Gallery
Page 62: William Dawson, *View of the Great Chasm of the Axmouth
    Landslip*, 1840. Philpot Museum, Lyme Regis
Page 70: Egdon Heath, Dorset
Pages 71–74: Extracts from Symphony No. 5 by Vaughan Williams
    © Oxford University Press 1946, reproduced by permission
Page 78: David Jones, *Vexilla Regis*, 1948, pencil and watercolour on
    paper, 30 × 22 in. Kettle's Yard, Cambridge
Page 84: Paul Nash, *Pillar and Moon*, 1932–42, oil on canvas, 20 × 30 in.
    Tate Gallery, London, reproduced by permission of Paul Nash Trust

Quotations
Page 15: John Constable in a letter to John Dunthorne, 29 May 1802
Page 23: John Ruskin, *Modern Painters*, Vol. I, Part II, 1843
Page 31: A. E. Housman, *A Shropshire Lad*, XLII, 1932
Page 39: Joachim Gasquet, *Cézanne: A Memoir with Conversations*,
    English edn tr. Christopher Pemberton, 1991; Andrew Causey, *Peter
    Lanyon*, 1971
Page 61: Edward Thomas, *Home*, from *Light and Twilight*, 1911
Page 69: W. H. Davies, *Leisure*, from *Songs of Joy and Others*, 1911
Page 77: Ralph Waldo Emerson, *Nature*, 1836; Henry David Thoreau,
    Walden, 1854
Page 83: Rosalind Thuillier, *Graham Sutherland: Inspirations*, 1982

Designed by Sally Jeffery
Printed in England by Balding + Mansell, Wisbech

CONTENTS

There are those who say, who is Cézanne? And those who say, so what about Cézanne anyway? The former don't know who he is even though nearly a hundred years ago he dragged us into the twentieth century virtually single-handed, visually at least. The latter would say he is history and so doesn't count.

But whether one accepts or rejects our modern world, there is also the rather elusive concept of Englishness. One asks, does it exist? Even, has it ever existed?

And there is, most importantly here, the question of landscape, our English landscape.

So many artists seem to be in search of a subject. I would suggest landscape: a subject full of eternal hope, great healing powers, phenomenal beauty, great mystery and with a wealth of history behind it – a subject on which artists, writers and composers, with all their fine modernist theories, can set to work.

The writers in this collection throw light on the subject from many angles, and the illustrations which follow the text survey the development of English landscape painting from Richard Wilson in the early eighteenth century to artists of the present day. Between the essays are ideas on the subject of landscape from historical writers.

The years 1750 to 1850 produced the first great age of English landscape painters; 1920 to 1960 produced another, with exceptional modernist language. Perhaps we could now enter yet another golden age.

The contributors to this book range from the youthful Adam Nicolson to the eminent Kathleen Raine: I thank them all. I hope it is an inspiration as much to the art lover as it is to the artist.   *Bernard Jacobson*

Gravetye Manor

Landscape: what is landscape good for? For all those ways of seeing: the visionary, the sublime, the realist, the historical, the quasi-erotic, the more simply physical, the scientific and the picturesque? I think so. But is there anything that goes beyond that all-too-modern democracy of styles? What is the under-structure of the landscape's attraction? There is a phrase here, quoted by David Matthews in his essay on the relationship of landscape and music, from Hardy's description of Egdon Heath. The heath, Hardy wrote in the first chapter of *The Return of the Native*, was 'a place perfectly accordant with man's nature – neither ghastly, hateful, nor ugly: neither commonplace, unmeaning nor tame; but like man, slighted and enduring'. Slighted and enduring! Those heroic adjectives, a nature that bears the marks of time and is indifferent to them. Perhaps that in the end is the underlying beauty of the landscape, its profoundly temporal nature and the way its seems to stand outside time.

I believe that but I doubt it too. Does landscape really have this supreme authority? Not everyone has always been convinced and the real landscape can be very disappointing. Hippolyte Taine, the French philosopher and historian, travelling to the Pyrenees in 1854, arrived at Biarritz to see the Atlantic Ocean, he says for the first time. 'I was most disagreeably disillusioned', Taine wrote. 'I seemed to be looking at one of those long stretches of turnip-fields that one sees in the country near Paris, intersected by patches of green cabbage, and strips of brownish barley. The distant sails looked like somebody's racing pigeons and even the view seemed rather narrow to me; painters had represented the sea as being much wider.' It was several days, he continued, before he could recover anything like a satisfactory 'sensation of immensity'.

Of course, Taine was not seeing the landscape. His disintegrated and dyspeptic glance out to sea settled on the diverse and constituent parts of ocean and shore, not on a landscape. Immensity takes some seeing. But what Taine, perhaps intuitively, understood, is that landscape does not exist; it can only be perceived. It is an aesthetic category not a thing and if, as Richard Mabey says in his essay here, the 'air of the salon' still hangs about the word, that is because no one ever digs the landscape or, as he falls into a peat-bog, damns the landscape for the dirt and the wet. Or to make the point more fiercely: no one would ever consider that the Moors Murderers (even if that particular catch-phrase depends on the long co-existence in the national mind of wild landscapes and brutality) had buried their victims in the landscape. They did that in pits a hundred yards or so from a Pennine road. Even to use the word in that context is somehow shocking and callous.

In the extremes of life, and in death, and when other more material things impinge, landscape ceases to be. But does that also mean that when art ceases to be polite, if *Mr and Mrs Andrews* does not represent everything that art might be, then landscape itself also falls away as a true subject for art?

That question, landscape's paradoxical combination of an insistent and an evanescent reality, of absolute presence and of being no more than a 'point of view', lies behind every one of the essays in this book and the practice of landscape art in the last two hundred years. But there is a further paradox in this: landscape's difficult status, its hesitant position between an objective reality and a subjective reshaping of the given world, has made it a peculiarly resonant medium for post-Romantic artists. Its own uncertain relationship to reality mimics the modern condition. We inhabit, in Christopher Neve's phrase, an unquiet landscape.

Again and again in the essays collected here, the suspicion nevertheless arises, explicitly or by implication, that landscape, in an era of abstraction and the international style, has become no more than a provincial form, a cosy backwater for those who cannot or will not engage with the problems and the challenge of modernism. Intriguingly, it is an anxiety that repeats Fuseli's sneer, quoted here by William Vaughan, that eighteenth-century English landscapes, compared with the grand forms of historical painting, were no more than 'the tame delineation of a given spot'. Consider the real world, the modern anti-landscapist will say, consider what has happened in it. Move your mind's eye from the bright and sonorous gaiety of *Dedham Lock* to the stirred up nightmare of Flanders mud, or Nash's *Totes Meer*, where the earth has become a sea of deathly and sickened unreliability, or to its human, peopled equivalent in *Guernica*. Where can landscape go after that if it is not to be anything but 'the tame delineation of a given spot', a

pretty view, the derogation of art's responsibilities? Won't all landscape, the sceptic asks, become the equivalent of Sunday painting after that? Or isn't retreat its only option, into the nearly comfortable landscape of Hockney's *Mr and Mrs Clark and Percy*, which is nothing in its flip insulation but the death of landscape, where Percy the shag-pile cat takes the place of the English hound and the shag-pile carpet stands in for England or even nature?

It is an attitude not to be dismissed. Geoffrey Hill has written:

I love my work and my children. God
Is distant, difficult. Things happen.
Too near the ancient troughs of blood
Innocence is no earthly weapon.

Because landscape, of its nature, is closely allied to innocence, to the hope of the innocence of Eden in a post-lapsarian world, the ferocious presence in our recent history of the ancient troughs of blood make the practice of landscape difficult. Landscape, far from engaging with them, can seem like a turning aside from the realities.

There is another problem. Read Thoreau now and his raging, teeming enthusiasm for the wild seems, like Geoffrey Hill's God, inaccessibly distant, difficult. 'In Wildness,' Thoreau wrote, 'is the preservation of the World. Every tree sends its fibres forth in search of the wild . . . I believe in the forest, and in the meadow, and in the night in which the corn grows . . . Give me wildness whose glance no civilisation can endure – as if we lived on the marrow of koodoos devoured raw.' Koodoos, those glamorous African animals, with their glamorous three-foot horns: it is not difficult to imagine that ingesting their marrow raw could seem like the ultimate in wild encounters.

But the twentieth century has seen enough of glances no civilisation could endure. As Norbert Lynton has so eloquently described here, the wild is now known to be at the heart of civilisation and the city threatens its inhabitants. The ancient troughs of blood are too easily to hand.

The landscape has traditionally provided two reservoirs of meaning – the innocent and the wild. Both have now been compromised by history. This is an impasse. Are there ways out of it?

There is one outstanding post-war English landscape poem which at least indicates a path that might be taken.

Philip Larkin published *The Whitsun Weddings* in 1964. It is, in its way, the archetype of the modern relation to landscape, a modern version of pastoral which understands the inaccessibility of innocence, its fragile, distant nature, but nevertheless makes its slow and graceful way towards that condition.

Larkin is travelling on a train from Hull to London. The air is hot, calm, Augustan. Larkin himself, book in hand, somehow resembles the figure of Brooke Boothby in the great painting by Wright of Derby, venturing into the landscape in his suit (Boothby holds a book labelled simply 'Rousseau' as he lies suited and a little awkwardly on the grass), continuing to read as England slips by. Even Larkin's train pursues an Augustan trajectory ('A slow and stopping curve southwards we kept') across Lincolnshire in the dreamy Whitsun heat. He hears people at each station making whoops and skirls but misinterprets them for porters larking with the mails and continues to read his book. But then his interest is roused, he looks out at the next station and sees it

> . . . all again in different terms:
> The fathers with broad belts under their suits
> And seamy foreheads; mothers loud and fat;
> An uncle shouting smut; and then the perms
> The nylon gloves and jewellery-substitutes,
> The lemons, mauves and olive-ochres that
>
> Marked off the girls unreally from the rest.

Larkin has now arrived in the landscape, it joins him in his carriage and he comes to see the couples who have just been married in a new light. From its distant, disengaged beginnings, the poem transforms — it is a majestic infusion of sympathetic humanity — as Larkin comes to understand how

> A dozen marriages got under way.
> They watched the landscape, sitting side by side
> An Odeon went past, a cooling tower,
> And someone running up to bowl —

The train comes into London and here the poem moves on again. The final transformation goes beyond human sympathy as a sudden, quite other-worldly beauty irrupts into the now-shared situation of Larkin and the newly married couples.

> We slowed again
> And as the tightened brakes took hold, there swelled

> A sense of falling, like an arrow-shower
> Sent out of sight, somewhere becoming rain.

In that last dropping away there is nothing triumphant, no golden revelation of a sudden happiness, but it does represent, in its strange and untranslatable imagery, a movement into another way of seeing, and a new serenity of understanding.

Larkin had begun the journey acutely aware of time ('That Whitsun I was late getting away: / Not till about / One-twenty on the sunlit Saturday / Did my three-quarters empty train pull out') and this in the casual voice of the everyday. By the end, in the heightened vocabulary of that arrow-rain shower, he has arrived in an almost Blakean other-world. This, if you want to isolate it, amounts to a definition of the Landscape Effect. The detailed, timetabled complexity becomes a kind of heavenly innocence. The journey ends up 'Annihilating all that's made / To a green thought in a green shade.' It is the innocence that comes with experience not the innocence before it. The marks that history has made on the landscape ('canals with floatings of industrial froth', 'acres of dismantled cars') are not ignored — as they would be in a sentimental version of this poem — but recognised and left, made redundant in the vision of human sympathy and the transmuted understanding (the ancestor of that final moment is in Henry Vaughan's 'I saw Eternity the other night') at which Larkin's train arrives.

For all the length and trajectory of this poem, landscape remains a lyric form. It is a moment of time in an extent of space. But the English landscape tradition is not the same as the Celtic or the Japanese. There is a complexity in its relationship to time. The picked haiku moment, the single flower seen in its isolation, the plop of the frog: that is scarcely what this tradition is about. That singularity may have appeared momentarily with Ruskin and the Pre-Raphaelites, with Rossetti's poem, for example, on the wood-spurge, but as William Vaughan says here, that way of seeing had few successors. This is not an imagiste sensibility. You can see that in Ivon Hitchens. Christopher Neve has described how Hitchens would place his canvases on the ground and lie down in front of them, painting the grass clumps, puddles and shadows immediately to hand. But if you didn't know that, you would never guess it. In the paintings themselves, the vision is encompassing, many-avenued, full of the dynamic of largeness and extent.

Perhaps the key figure in this is Wordsworth, who, as Norbert Lynton describes here, walks for tens of thousands of miles, most of them on the public roads which he preferred to mountain paths for their regularity and the way in which they allowed the momentum of thought to unroll without interruption, 'building moments of perception into monuments of considered experience'. That sense of building, that robust folding and kneading of time into the work of art is central to the English landscape tradition. It does not exist through time but it is of time.

Connections resonate across this landscape community. Wordsworth on the continuous road; Larkin's slow, preparatory curve across England; Ben Nicholson discussing his own work, if at all, not in terms of influences on him or the meaning of what he is doing, but of ping-pong and dancing, the curve of the spun ball and the perfect execution of a turning, dancing step; Edward Thomas dedicating a book to his friend Harry Hooton, saying to him that 'the end is in the means – in the sight of that beautiful long straight line of the Downs in which a curve is latent'. And that curve reappears in William Tillyer's recent landscapes, the curve of classical form, the clarity and poise of order against the enriched and vital turbulence of the paint beside them, so precisely described here by Nicholas Alfrey as 'imagined spaces generated by the flow and drag of pigment across a surface'.

Is this curve, the classical disciplining form of it, the curve of time contained? It seems tempting to say so and, if it is, the English landscape becomes a lyric-narrative, a place outside time in which the passage of time is somehow contained. Look, say, at Stanley Spencer's painting of the May Tree at Cookham. The revelatory presence of the tree is almost overloaded with its own flowering vitality. Its blossom is on the point of merging with the clouds. There is nothing wan or haiku-ish here. This is the natural world in trumpets. And its place, carefully and minutely depicted along the foot of the picture, guarantees the unworldly phenomenon of the tree a foothold in the world of time passing. All the elements of the real landscape, as described here by Richard Mabey, are folded into the depicted moment.

We cannot remember duration. All we can remember is the place in which time occurred. The landscape, in fact, stands for memory. It is the means by which time is fixed. As Gaston Bachelard wrote in *The Poetics of Space*: 'In its countless alveoli, space contains compressed time. That is what space is for.' Landscape consists of the countless inflected spaces which the stream of time creates. Archaeology and fossil hunting are only the most explicit forms of remembering that we have. The dream-positioning of Surrealist globes and objects in the landscape in some of the pale, chalky paintings done by Paul Nash in the 1930s is matched calmly enough in others done at the same time by the standing stones of Avebury or the chalk figures inscribed in the turf of the Downs. These marks and objects are as arbitrary in their way as the geometrical figures but they are also more than that. Without effort the stones and the turf-cut giants are part both of the seen landscape and of the landscape of common memory, the unconscious made tangible.

The language itself recognises landscape as the ground of meaning, not only in poetry ('the expense of spirit in a waste of shame', 'Come in under this red rock') but in our everyday usage. To place something, to feel at home with it, to be unsettled, upset or even all at sea, to have one's feet on the ground or one's head in the air – these are to take up positions within the landscape. In its etymology, even understanding itself is a landscape event. Understanding, if you look at the word before the metaphor took control of it, is to put the whole of one's body under something. There is a sense in which to abandon all the access to meaning that landscape provides, as so many modernists have insisted, would be to abandon an important part of meaning itself.

Nicholas Alfrey suggests in his essay here that for many contemporary painters 'Abstract Expressionism was where real painting started' and that, however short a phenomenon Abstract Expressionism itself was, it provided the way forward for landscape painting. Nothing in the pages that follow here is more suggestive or optimistic than that idea of revitalising the landscape tradition through a radical turning aside. It is not a turning aside towards the sentimental or the scholastic but, in Alfrey's words, towards 'the direct engagement with materials, not bounded by the constraints of description, invention or abstraction'.

That sentence would fit a way of treating landscape itself. The landscape does not have to be a historical, an economic, a commercial or, in its conventional sense, an aesthetic thing. With all the directness, physicality and unzipped energy of the abstract expressionists, it can become a physical experience. And that is when it can be rediscovered as source of vitality and beauty. A real engagement with the landscape involves the sort of shrugging away of emotional distance that Larkin enacts so beautifully in *The Whitsun Weddings*.

Both Margaret Drabble and Norbert Lynton speak in these pages of the underlying sexuality of the relationship to the landscape and there is no doubt in my mind of the truth of that thought, above all in the sweat and exhaustion of a long day in the field, in the drugged sensuality of deep physical tiredness, in the sort of broken, stimulating immediacy of physical experience recorded for example in Coleridge's Westmorland Journals.

Paul Barker may well be right in saying that the holiest shrine in England is the law of contract, but property evaporates in the light of what could be called, in this deeply engaged sense, True Landscape. Perhaps that is what gives trespass its deep and lasting pleasure, its neglect of the historical and legal framework in claiming the unmediated reality of landscape for oneself. And trespass, the alertness it summons, the attention to surrounding detail it requires, the sense of being in the world so strangely heightened that it gives you – this may well be the model on which the new landscape can be founded. Be like a trespasser in the landscape and you will inevitably see it for new.

It is worth thinking of Maurice Cockrill in this light, his garnering, spacious, cumulative, sudden vision. Look at his paintings and you will find a piece from here and there. It is not the view from the hill which Richard Mabey sees as responsible for so much that is wrong in the way the English have seen the landscape, but the view from within it. Cockrill is a poacher as much as a trespasser, a man to whom the landscape belongs, as it did to John Clare, more than to the man who, by the sacred law of contract, was said to own it.

The picturesque tradition of landscape denies this inner and subversive vividness, the intimacy of contact, because it imposes an agreed way of seeing things on the reality we need to experience unclothed. And anyway we know it to be untrue. As Richard Jefferies wrote in the 1880s:

So many pictures and so many illustrations seem to proceed upon the assumption that steam-plough and reaping machine do not exist, that the landscape contains nothing but what it did a hundred years ago. These sketches are often beautiful, but they lack the force of truth and reality. Every one who has been fifty miles into the country, if only by rail, knows while looking at them that they are not real. You feel there is something wanting, you do not know what. That something is the hard, perhaps angular fact which at once makes the sky above it appear likewise a fact.

And the facts that have to be accounted for now are not simply the presence of reaping machines and fast-dry silo systems but the revolution in art and thought that has taken place this century. Landscape has to absorb modernism; it cannot ignore it.

It may be difficult, as Kathleen Raine suggests here in her essay on the spirituality of landscape, to transmute cows, to give cows, as David Jones found, a satisfactorily Platonic quality. But perhaps that Platonic idea, of somehow lifting cows into their higher selves, has become rather a dead end. It has about it, however unlikely a connection this might sound, something of the quality of Horace Walpole's dainty remarks on the English landscape, quoted here by Margaret Drabble. The real thing was far too *rainy* 'so that an observation I made forty years ago, is most true, that this country exhibits the most beautiful landscapes in the world when they are framed and glazed, that is, when you look at them through the window'.

That ranking of the transmuted and the untransmuted cow, the real landscape and the glazed, was left behind by the Romantics, for whom, in a grand political vision of liberty, barriers and classifications were burnt away. For Baudelaire immensity and intimacy had become the same thing: a few lines by Liszt, he wrote in *L'art romantique*, gave him 'one of those impressions of happiness that nearly all imaginative men have experienced in their sleeping dreams. I felt freed from *the powers of gravity*, and, through memory, succeeded in recapturing the extraordinary *voluptuousness* that pervades *high places*.

Involuntarily, I pictured to myself the delightful state of a man in the grip of a long daydream, in absolute solitude, but a solitude with an *immense horizon* and widely diffused light; in other words, immensity with no other setting than itself.' That is the classic statement of the Romantic landscape – spacious, happy, beautiful, widely lit, infused with voluptuousness, and sharing the intimacy and privacy of the real with the immensity of the abstract.

It is intriguing that Baudelaire's description should be of a landscape that is at once musical, visual, verbal and physical. Landscape, as a subject, has had a way over the last three or four centuries of migrating from one of these zones to another. The expressive landscape had appeared in poetic language ('the multitudinous seas incarnadine') at a time when the painted landscape had scarcely separated itself from the estate survey. The Romantic period saw a unique flowering of landscape art in virtually every form. But by the end of that century, the painted landscape had sunk back towards the picturesque. Just then, however, as David Matthews describes here, it was entering its most fruitful period in music. Was it that only music could take up where Turner had left off? And

that only when the plastic arts had moved towards a more musical, abstract condition themselves could landscape flood back into the art of Nicholson, Moore and their contemporaries?

Whatever its particular outlet, its mouth into the sea of consciousness, the fat river of landscape meaning will not be suppressed. The scientific approaches of ecology and landscape history may buttress the essential understanding that landscape brings but they will not replace it. That core is the vitality to be found there, the juiciness of life. Norbert Lynton remarks that both Turner and Constable enjoyed the *moistness* of the landscape. That is the right word. It is the wetness that is to be welcomed and not glazed away: Walpole's shuddered-at drizzle becomes Constable's wettened, glistening trees, is glimpsed in Eliot's desperate call in *The Waste Land* for 'even the sound of water' and reappears in Larkin's unexpected blessing of a distant shower. Landscape does mix memory and desire and does stir dull roots with spring rain. It remains the source of a refreshing interflood between the self and the world.

Adam Nicolson

There is room enough for a natural painture. The great vice of the present day is *bravura*, an attempt at something beyond the truth . . . *Fashion* always had, & will have its day – but *Truth* (in all things) only will last and can have just claims on posterity.

John Constable

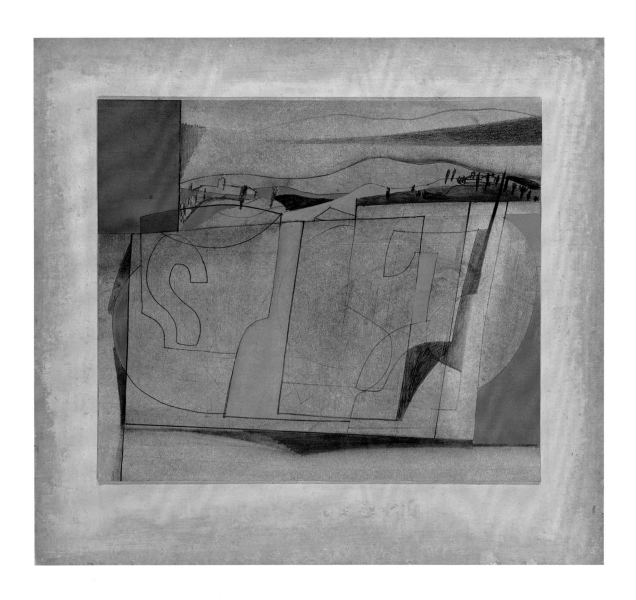

Ben Nicholson *Tuscany* 1951

LANDSCAPE AFTER BATTLE

The field of Waterloo is a field of mercy to ours.

Constable's bitter words are a reminder that landscape painting was experienced as a desperate business, even in what has come to seem in retrospect the golden age of the art in England. Constable had to battle against indifference and scepticism in order to establish ordinary landscape as a valid subject for serious painting. Full recognition of his achievement came only after his death, and landscape eventually came to occupy a privileged place in English art. But landscape painters have only rarely enjoyed the benefits of unbroken peace; difficulty and uncertainty have often been attendant on the art, and Constable was by no means the last to have to fight for its very existence.

Landscape painting is as marginal now, arguably, as it ever was in Constable's day. Landscape is often seen as peripheral to the concerns of progressive art, and the label 'landscape painter' is one that few contemporary artists have been anxious to embrace. The rise of modernism has tended to displace landscape as a viable practice. Some have countered by maintaining that the English landscape tradition can be interpreted in modernist terms, while others have appealed to it as an alternative to modernism. There may be something insubstantial and ambiguous about the very nature of that tradition, however, which makes it less than secure as a point of departure.

Why should landscape have become ever more awkward terrain to negotiate? This essay does not attempt a chronological survey of the rise, decline, survival or transformation of landscape. It is concerned rather with landscape as an uncertain legacy, with how little of the past can be recovered and how much has been lost or misread.

There has always been a tendency to undervalue landscape, or else to load it with fantasies of Englishness. The task of coming to a better historical understanding of the genre is always in progress, but it is also possible to assert a belief in the future of landscape painting, and to argue for its inexhaustible scope. The two projects are not necessarily connected. What is vital in contemporary landscape painting need not derive exclusively from any native antecedent. To invoke the British tradition is no guarantee of value; a painting regenerated by the modernism of mid-century, however, is more likely to have the means and the confidence to embark on a rediscovery of the potential of landscape.

DESERT, ASCENDANCY

The history of English landscape painting since the early nineteenth century only exists in fragments: there is no definitive account of the subject as a whole. Why should the subject have proved so difficult to chronicle? This missing history should at least be a warning to anyone seeking to assert the reassuring existence of a native landscape tradition, against which painting can be measured and to which it might return.

In the vacuum left by the absence of any Authorised Version of landscape history, a number of artists and writers have woven the theme into surveys of their own. John Piper, Michael Ayrton, Kenneth Clark, Nikolaus Pevsner, Geoffrey Grigson and Peter Fuller have all made the attempt. Some recurring preoccupations run through these accounts: the defence of a painting culture with a low self-image, frequently overwhelmed by outside influence; the attempt to define Englishness, and to identify native characteristics and strengths. The resulting play of insight, distortion and special pleading over the field of landscape has been both richly suggestive and deeply misleading.

Desert, ascendancy: the terms are borrowed from Michael Ayrton, who first applied them in 1946 to the subject of British drawing; they are adopted here because of the wider resonances they suggest. An image of emptiness is juxtaposed with one of power to convey a vivid sense of British art as drastically uneven, veering between extremes. The model implied here is a cyclical one, with brief bursts of achievement and longer phases of vacancy. Landscape is implicated in this, sometimes powerfully in the ascendant, but often merely barren and empty.

One of the deserts bleakly pointed to by Ayrton was the Victorian period; here the rich inheritance of Romanticism was somehow squandered. But nothing could more clearly demonstrate than this verdict the lack of consensus as to what is worth doing in landscape, and what is worth holding on to. The desert turns out to include Pre-Raphaelitism, and therefore some of the most extraordinary and memorable of English landscape paintings. Who would now wish to write off so many compressed, hallucinatory and uncompromising pictures, intensely engaged with place, yet still concerned with technical and formal innovation? Taste and chance have occluded so much of what has been done in landscape. Ruskin had believed he was witnessing the establishment of a new and brilliant British school, but it did not prove as durable as he hoped. No subsequent painting could build on this exacting vision, and twentieth-century painters grew up assuming that the great tradition of landscape had long since died out.

As for ascendancy, there was never any doubt that this meant the Romantic movement; indeed when the idea of the English tradition is invoked this is often what it really comes down to. Gradually it came to acquire such legendary dimension that it seemed to contain the key to any revival of the spirit of British art. Only by acknowledging what had been achieved could Britain hope to recover confidence and identity. Ayrton and Piper wrote in the belief that an artistic renaissance in Britain would emerge from the devastation of the Second World War; this would be a new phase in a cycle last in the ascendant in the great years of Romanticism, and, as in those earlier war years, genuine artistic achievement would be born out of national pride and cultural isolation.

What is striking about the Neo-Romanticism of the 1940s and early 1950s, however, is how reduced and narrow the language of landscape had become. Little could be made of Turner, but much of Palmer. Invention and linearity are the predominant values, perhaps because they are those most compatible with the example of Picasso. There is a drift towards mannerism, and to eccentric mysticism. Despite the rhetoric of those who set store by the 'welling up of an indigenous Romantic sensibility', too often Neo-Romanticism offers a pinched and disappointing flowering.

In the end, the idea of an English Romantic tradition, lost by the mid-nineteenth century but regained in the mid-twentieth, does not make a convincing framework within which to make sense of landscape painting. Neo-Romanticism affords only the most unreliable glimpses of

the movement from which it takes its name, while much that is interesting in twentieth-century landscape cannot be associated with it. Neither Bomberg nor Hitchens has any part in it, for example, though the latter was able to make a better use of Turner than any self-avowed Neo-Romantic.

LIMITS OF VISION

A striking feature of the British tradition as it was conceived in the twentieth century is that many of the artists who made it up were held to be ahead of their time, or at least unsuccessful in their day or misunderstood by their contemporaries. Artists with an innovative, experimental approach were thus privileged and, as an inevitable corollary, many of the achievements that were once valued became lost to sight. Landscape painting lies right at the heart of this process of recovery and loss: a few isolated, uncompromising figures were highlighted, while whole reaches of the landscape tradition were dismissed or forgotten. The motivation for all this was doubtless an understandable need to assert the vitality of native art against a powerful and progressive European painting, though it sometimes comes across as a critical fantasy projected back into the past to compensate for the poor showing of a British avant-garde in later years. But any tradition created in such a selective and ahistorical way is bound to prove unstable.

Certain artists of the Romantic period acquired an afterlife in which the significance of their work was subtly recast or entirely reinvented. Turner's is the most striking case, though other reputations could also be invested with a retrospective clarity. So Cotman's art emerged as hard-edged and crystal-clear, even proto-abstract, though he had once been undervalued in both his native city and the capital, and his career was but a series of culs-de-sac. Palmer's reputation (one decade of against-the-grain achievement traded in for the entire balance of a respectable career) is reinforced by a potent counter-myth of the sudden loss of vision and a fall into conformity and materialism. Constable could be claimed as the true precursor of Impressionism, and thus enlisted to sustain a myth of French initiative and the failure of the Victorians to recognise real painting. His sketches from nature and his expressionistic handling were held up as signs of artistic integrity, but his big set pieces were increasingly left to populists and historians; it would be the latter who would eventually succeed in restoring a disturbing edge to the exhibited pastorals by making them into an ideological battle-ground.

In the case of Turner, historians and artists have been talking at cross purposes for years. No matter how assiduously scholars have endeavoured to discredit the notion that Turner's real subject was light, or even paint, his reputation outside specialist circles still rests on his enigmatic late canvases, his works-in-progress and his private notes, such as those he made at Petworth. There may be every reason to be sceptical about claims that Turner paves the way for Impressionism, Symbolism and even Abstract Expressionism, but these are still the ways in which later painters have persisted in trying to make sense of his work. The formidable density of reference in his pictures and their complex levels of meaning have produced many academic commentaries but no artistic progeny.

Turner made of landscape something potentially encyclopaedic in scope, though not necessarily large in scale; indeed it has been argued that he only fully expresses himself on paper rather than canvas. The wider context, at least initially, for his transformation of landscape was the Napoleonic wars: a Britain isolated, blockaded and turned in upon itself. Turner's response to these constraints was twofold: fantasies of an unreachable Europe, and especially Italy, on the one hand, and an intense scrutiny of the homeland on the other. His English scenes were made to carry an increasing burden of knowledge, and diverse kinds of observation – geological, antiquarian, social, botanical, whimsical – were plotted out across his compositions.

The need to extend the range of landscape to encompass new perceptions of nature has an obvious parallel in contemporary development in the natural sciences. Such an enterprise will inevitably have very little place for the merely picturesque, and the limitations of the existing pictorial conventions quickly become exposed. A dynamic, expanded conception of landscape necessitates a rethinking of relations within the picture field. The framing edge becomes progressively less important in defining the scope of a view; picture space is radically deepened, and the eye offered a choice of

several routes through it; spaces are elided so as to produce dense conjunctions of imagery. The brush-mark takes on an abrupt, provisional, unstable character, as if to suggest the action of complex forces. There is a direct relationship, therefore, between this spate of formal invention and the forging of a more comprehensive account of the workings of landscape.

Various aspects of this formidable battery of innovations have been isolated since, and held up for admiration, though rarely with much regard for the vast system of which they formed a part. Very little of that ambitious project to enhance the capabilities of landscape survived into the next generation. Turner's own later pictures, admittedly, were sufficiently enigmatic to balk any obvious succession. But after mid-century, the possibilities of landscape appear to recede. There was still much talk of the inroads of the scientific spirit, and the responsibilities of painting to give a precise account of the natural world; but the limits of this world had contracted, and Ruskin encouraged artists to engage with landscape at obsessively close range. In the same period, there was also a revival of the values of an older, less analytical school, and the apparatus of the picturesque was gradually restored to working order. Landscape became once again the domain of the merely and exclusively pictorial.

Landscape painting had been, for a time, a central, innovative, energetic discipline, but gradually reverted to being a specialised and respectable branch of the profession: by the twentieth century it was an intermittent and marginal genre once more. There are so many possible explanations for its decline. Its well-being had long been bound up with the practice of water-colour, but the medium gradually lost its old prestige and became the preserve of the amateur and conservative. The physical landscape itself was widely perceived as degenerating, becoming unpaintable, breaking down into a series of zones of blight, intensive farming and artificially maintained enclaves of natural beauty. Landscape painting became inexorably associated with nostalgia and escapism.

A sense of what had once been achieved in landscape persisted, and even grew stronger. But it also narrowed drastically, until the confines of Palmer's valley came to count for as much as Turner's dense, wheeling prospects.

HEARTLAND

The English landscape has been gradually lost to one kind of painting and claimed by another. Traditionalists have flourished in the territory given up by artists committed to a progressive approach. The artists occupying this middle ground are content to continue working in a naturalistic idiom, and to leave modern art to its own unnatural devices. Such artists are backed by their own institutions and have their own networks of support and patronage. They see themselves as the true heirs to a great tradition abandoned by the moderns in their restless search for novelty. Central to this tradition is the 'English' art of water-colour; in this context the idea of tradition does have an undeniable coherence, since it refers unambiguously to an artistic succession (Cozens, Girtin, Cotman, de Wint, Cox) and holds up a clearly defined body of work as a source of inspiration and authority.

Traditional landscape has several strong cards to play: it offers pleasure, profit, a ready market and a deeper sense of belonging. There is, for example, the appeal of sketching from nature, with all its connotations of health, directness and authenticity. The emphasis on the didactic aspect is especially striking. The lessons of twentieth-century landscape masters are conveyed in innumerable 'how to' books and manuals, just as were the lessons of their nineteenth-century predecessors like Cox. Such books might seem to display sheer virtuosity for admiration rather than help the reader master the art in practice. But, by systematically laying out the various techniques and tricks of the trade, they do at least encourage a full and discriminating appreciation of the art. The cultivation of both method and spontaneity is emphasised, but so too is the pleasure to be gained from the exercise, and the potential rewards, both spiritual and material. A ready market is guaranteed by the overlapping interest groups of tourism and local pride. Modernist art is, by contrast, difficult, angst-ridden, unteachable and hard to sell.

Can there be any kind of relationship between Romantic landscape, conservative tradition and modernism? As an example of how some complex transactions are played out over a symbolic terrain, take the case of Rowland Hilder, Graham Sutherland and the area around Shoreham in north Kent, once so closely associated with Palmer in his visionary years. Hilder is the dean of traditionalists, whose best known work, the *Garden of England*, depicting a winding Kentish lane, oast houses and a cluster of farmsteads, is a veritable icon of the south country. Hilder and Sutherland, contemporaries and fellow students, belong to the generation who discovered Palmer in the 1920s, and both make frequent and explicit references to him in their work. Yet Hilder's bland, nostalgic pastorals entirely efface Palmer's Shoreham; moreover, he has been content to allow his admirers to coin the term 'Hilderscape' to refer to a certain kind of Kentish landscape in a pointed appropriation for traditionalism. With Sutherland, Palmer's inspiration leads in a very different direction: at first archaic and fey, but gradually darker, more intense, and altogether less reassuring.

For all their confident claims to have recovered the true paths of landscape, the traditionalists are haunted nevertheless by a sense of exclusion. They are ignored by the critics, unrepresented in national collections and written out of accounts of twentieth-century art. The traditionalists have committed themselves to the defence of a landscape heartland of their own invention, but have managed to persuade only fellow travellers that their vision is tenable or worthwhile.

The modernists, for their part, have only intermittently engaged with landscape. No common stylistic approach links the work of artists like Bomberg, Nicholson, Nash, Hitchens, Sutherland or Lanyon, except a desire to acknowledge the range of formal innovations developed elsewhere in the twentieth century. Landscape is filtered, refracted or disrupted, the eye continually held up at the surface. The tone is often ambiguous or enigmatic, the mood theatrical or exaggerated, characterised by sudden lyrical bursts or the suggestion of an ominous undertow.

Traditionalists and modernists have incompatible visions of landscape to offer: on the one hand, nostalgia, the picturesque, the timeless values of the countryside; on the other, a landscape of our time, tainted, fitful and unquiet. Both appeal to some notion of a British tradition, and both seek to use the past as an authority. Sometimes the same name will be invoked on both sides: Constable, for example, can stand either as a model of uncompromising naturalism or of expressive force. But the opposition between these visions is deeply misleading. Their nineteenth-century predecessors were capable of encompassing, within a single frame, both naturalism and formal innovation, celebration and anxiety. It is only in the fracturing of that complex, multi-levelled whole that landscape is diminished.

UNDISCOVERED COUNTRY

Despite the burden of the preceding sections, it is nevertheless possible to conclude by declaring that landscape painting is by no means played out. Landscape may have become uncertain ground for the artist, and the idea of tradition unravels under scrutiny. But there are still painters who have found convincing and original ways of engaging with landscape; there is no reason to doubt that the genre will continue to be extended. To take this position necessarily involves the defence of painting itself as an activity, as opposed to those other forms of art practice in which landscape is variously documented, intervened in, marked out or treated as an arena for performance. It is still possible to envisage a landscape painting that is completely consistent with modernism.

As modernism intensified its hold on both the practice and criticism of painting, its growing antipathy to landscape also became more clear. In its earlier stages, up to Cézanne and Fauvism, modernism had a use for landscape. But as the 'proper' concerns of painting became ever more rigorously defined, a process culminating with Abstract Expressionism, those who continued to draw on landscape were made to seem compromised and provincial. A hardline approach demanded the progressive stripping away of illusionism and association in order to clarify painting's essential resources: gesture, the physical properties of paint, the flatness of the surface, colour. That the process revitalised painting, there can be no question; its positive effects have long outlasted the relatively brief period of Abstract Expressionism's prestige. It would be misleading to present modernism as a set of restrictive practices. Once

seeming to foreclose on landscape, in the longer run it allowed the opening up of a new world. This world is made visible through the direct engagement with materials, and is not bounded by the constraints of description, invention or abstraction. Its potential is rich enough to suggest that what has been realised so far are but the bare lineaments of an undiscovered country.

It would be idle to speculate as to whether British painting ever had the potential to renew itself from within; it would be equally futile to base any account of British art on the alleged superiority of the native tradition over alien forms. Few painters whose careers have begun since the early 1960s have been unaffected by the American example in some degree, and for many Abstract Expressionism was where real painting started. The debate as to whether British art was impoverished or enriched by this is likely to be needlessly divisive. Much more to the point is to show how a regenerated painting can provide the means with which to address the issue of place and experience; it can even provide a vantage point from which to come to new terms with the recent past of British art itself.

Landscape in the work of painters like William Tillyer and Maurice Cockrill is not defined by the line of a horizon or a fixed viewpoint. These are imagined spaces, generated by the flow and drag of pigment across a surface, sequences of light and shadow which also register unequivocally as a series of direct painterly gestures. These fields of marks are activated by a network of references and allusions, and in this respect are reminiscent of a vein of Romantic landscape from Cozens to Turner. The paintings may be full of echoes, but they are not sustained by any sense of an enduring landscape tradition.

These are landscapes in the idiom of our time, built up from a complex overlay of direct study, distant memory, inherited imagery and formal strategy. They encompass both wilderness and exploited ground, artifice and disorder, delicacy and disruption. One kind of landscape may gradually have become unpaintable in our century, but another is already taking shape. No map can give access to the terrain it discloses.

The noonday sun came slanting down the rocky slopes of La Riccia, and their masses of entangled and tall foliage, whose autumnal tints were mixed with the wet verdure of a thousand evergreens, were penetrated with it as with rain. I cannot call it colour, it was conflagration. Purple, and crimson, and scarlet, like the curtains of God's Tabernacle, the rejoicing trees sank into the valley in showers of light, every separate leaf quivering with buoyant and burning life; each, as it turned to reflect or to transmit the sunbeam, first a torch and then an emerald. Far up into the recesses of the valley, the green vistas arched like the hollows of mighty waves of some crystalline sea, with the arbutus flowers dashed along their flanks for foam, and silver flakes of orange spray tossed into the air around them, breaking over the grey walls of rock into a thousand separate stars, fading and kindling alternately as the weak wind lifted and let them fall. Every glade of grass burned like the golden floor of heaven, opening in sudden gleams as the foliage broke and closed above it, as sheet-lightning opens in a cloud at sunset; the motionless masses of dark rock — dark though flushed with scarlet lichen, casting their quiet shadows across its restless radiance, the fountain underneath them filling its marble hollow with blue mist and fitful sound; and over all, the multitudinous bars of amber and rose, the sacred clouds that have no darkness, and only exist to illumine, were seen in fathomless intervals between the solemn and orbed repose of the stone pines, passing to lose themselves in the last, white, blinding lustre of the measureless line where the Campagna melted into the blaze of the sea.

John Ruskin

The stones of England   *Paul Barker*

Salle Church, Norfolk

You come over the brow of one of Norfolk's low hills, in that north-eastern corner of the county which, in winter especially, feels to be countless miles from anywhere. You have slipped into another time, and you find yourself humming a hymn tune as you drive:

A thousand ages in Thy sight
Are like an evening gone . . .

Then, there it is, the tall grey west tower of Salle church. It points skywards, like the finger of God. Nothing quite prepares you for it, in this landscape of narrow roads, occasional farmhouses, small deciduous woods, and the big, dominating prairie fields of modern (and medieval) agriculture. Salle church stands now, as it must have stood when it was first built in the early fifteenth century, a sudden vertical insert into the horizontals of East Anglia. For perhaps two hundred years, a net of hedgerows spread all round it, softening the landscape, and softening the impact of that 127-foot tower. No longer.

England tends towards cosiness, given half a chance. But Salle was built in the full-throated pride of an emergent middle class. These men, squeezing their capital out of the wool trade, made England the first bourgeois state. They stamped their favourite (and purely English) style, the Perpendicular, all over the landscape that had enriched them. One of the biggest of the wool churches is at Worstead (hence, worsted), a few miles away. But nowhere in Norfolk outranks Salle. It was built as Harfleur was besieged and the battle of Agincourt fought, and it bears Henry V's coat of arms. Geoffrey Boleyn is buried here (he had bought a local estate from Sir John Fastolf); a hundred years later, his unmarried, pregnant great-granddaughter, Anne, and another Henry, precipitated the English Reformation.

Perpendicular is so tied, in memory and imagination, with the Anglican church (Dissenters, and the revived Roman Catholic church, avoided it) that it is hard to remember that it wasn't always so. Perhaps architecture, here, helped give birth to change. This is not the architecture of homage to Rome. It is the architecture of pride of place, and this meant 'place' in both the geographical and social senses: God for Harry, England and the local gentry.

Even before the iconoclasts came round with their hammers, Perpendicular churches were always clear-lit, even harsh, inside. They are big, and, like a cinema or a skyscraper, the bigger they are, the better their architecture works. Over on the Norfolk coast, at Happisburgh church, you can hear and see the waves of the North Sea, only a few yards away, through the Puritan-plain glass windows. But at Salle, as in almost every other Perpendicular church anywhere in England, you see sky, and from certain positions trees and grass. The landscape penetrates into these churches as, later, it also penetrated through the clear glass of rationalist Georgian naves and chancels, in the next flurry of middle-class church building. By contrast, the landscape of the outside world did not reach into the earlier, more inward (or upward) looking Gothic churches, their narrow windows screened with stained glass; or into the revived, anxious, Gothic gloom of Victorian England.

It is always called 'Salle church' (pronounced Saul), not 'St Peter and St Paul'. It is the church that defines the place. There is no visible village; only a few houses. The architecture of the church demarcates this landscape. What matters, as you look, is how everything relates to that tower and its wheeling rooks. It has outlasted the doctrines it was designed for, and the population. The landscape, these past few years, has settled back into something closer to the way it was in the early fifteenth century; Norfolk, like the rest of East Anglia, is becoming more populous again; and who can tell what will happen to the Church of England? The architecture, meanwhile, has borne its own kind of witness to what 'Salle' meant, regardless.

On this winter's day, the clock is stopped at ten past seven. The sun etches the angles of the tower. As you get nearer, you see a circular concrete water-holder, on stilts, beyond the church; but this anonymous official amenity brings no special definition to its surroundings. As you walk through the lych-gate, the tower becomes more and more vertiginous. Dorothy Edith Merian was buried in the graveyard in 1988, aged eighty-one; Bessie Easter Eke in 1978, aged seventy-nine. Like the church itself, they have become part of the landscape.

England (leaving aside Scotland and Wales) is the most densely populated country in Europe, more crowded even than Holland. Its landscape has been invented, and constantly reinvented, by its inhabitants. It has scarcely any terrain you could even begin to call a wilderness.

The grandeur of the Yorkshire Dales is inseparable now from the eighteenth and nineteenth century dry-stone walls, thrown like a net over even the most Gulliveresque hills: this is the landscape of Parliamentary Enclosure. No English landscape can be understood without considering its history of ownership and use. But, equally, it cannot be understood without its architecture.

Architecture is the clearest statement the landscape contains. It announces, with primitive pride of possession: 'This land is mine (and not yours)'; 'This is my house'; 'This is my God (and should be yours)'. To these assertions, with time, are added others, not dissimilar: 'This is my corn mill', evolving into 'This is my cotton factory'. As finance grows cannier, a certain impersonality starts to creep in: 'This is the company's canal (or railway)'. This is followed, historically, by the grandeur of early public service: '*our* reservoir, *our* gas-holder, *our* workhouse, *our* infirmary'. But 'ours' still does not mean 'everyone's'. Manchester turned Haweswater, in the Lake District, into a reservoir to supply the city's homes and factories with water. In pursuit of the greatest good of the greatest number, it drowned the local villagers' church of Holy Trinity, at Mardale. The Piranesian stonework of the reservoir is an unabashed homage to the Utilitarian power of Manchester corporation in its heyday.

We continue to throw new nets over the countryside. (This was one of the things D. H. Lawrence so disliked about England.) Dry-stone walling is perhaps mere masonry. But few other nets are so untouched by formal architecture. When the Post Office spread out its telephone lines over the country, and built local call-boxes, it turned to Giles Gilbert Scott, the architect of the Gothic Anglican cathedral in Liverpool (and later, of Battersea power station), who modelled the classic red cast-iron booth on John Soane's neo-classical memorial to his wife, in the churchyard of old St Pancras church, behind St Pancras Station. When the new Central Electricity Board began to create its national supply grid, and wanted to make its pylons look respectable, it turned to bluff Reginald Blomfield, architect of the rebuilt Quadrant at Piccadilly Circus, of The Headrow at Leeds and of the grandiose Menin Gate war memorial at Ypres.

Little is unplanned about the English landscape, and its architectural component underlines this. Exceptions prove the rule. Even more than the spread of Voysey-derived semi-detached suburbs between the world wars, the so-called 'plotland' intrusion of completely unplanned architecture threw the powers-that-be into panic, and gave rise to our present planning legislation. In south Essex, and along the Channel coast from Brighton, people began to build their own houses, often little more than shacks. East of Brighton, the settlement of Peacehaven became notorious among country-lovers: it made it even harder to peer across the South Downs without seeing a bungalow. In Essex, the plotlands are directly responsible for the location of the New Town of Basildon. Only with the powers, and finance, that a New Town gave them, could officials demolish thousands of do-it-yourself homes. They had produced a landscape more American than English. It was erased.

Ours is a landscape of control. One of the wonders of Britain is its Ordnance Survey maps. The survey was started, as the gunmaster name implies, for military purposes. On every hilltop now, there sits a mini-obelisk with a brass bevel in the top, for the surveyors to fix their theodolites. But trig points, with their War Ministry arrowhead symbol imprinted in the concrete, are no longer needed for modern mapping. To my eye they have always eroded any sense of isolation in the places where they are built. You might as well put a garden gnome on the top of Scafell Pike. But it turns out that they have grown into people's affections. Like red telephone boxes (though not, so far as I know, pylons), they generated a campaign to conserve them. The English countryside needs its architecture.

I grew up in a Pennine valley, which at the time was dotted with small, thriving mill towns. I found it especially hard here to think of landscape as something without buildings in it. In a valley called Jumble Hole Clough, the chimneys of dead mills (built here for the water power, then killed by coal) poked up through the trees. Where streams came off the moor and started to plunge down the valley sides, there were (and are) small hump-backed packhorse bridges, so changeless that they can be impossible to give a date to. On one of the highest moors, visible from all around, rose the rain and soot blackened obelisk of Stoodley Pike. It was put there by the cotton manufacturers of Todmorden as a thanksgiving for the brief Peace of Amiens, in 1802, which interrupted the Napoleonic wars, and allowed English cloth into the Continent again. The obelisk's heavy Egyptian lineaments bear witness to the manufacturers' Masonic connections, as well as to their love of free trade. But the peace didn't last, and lightning kept striking the obelisk (which is so large you can go up inside it, if you can stand the walk to the moor top). But Napoleon was finally defeated, and Stoodley Pike was rebuilt. The Pike and, on an opposing hillside, a ruined church (which as children we were always told, wrongly, had been destroyed by Cromwell's troops): these gave this landscape its trademark. Without them, it would have lacked identity; it might have been almost any upper Pennine valley on the millstone-grit measures.

The architectural evidence of the past is everywhere around you in the English landscape. Leaving aside the obvious divergences of climate and geology, this marks it off from, say, Germany or Israel. Countries like these have been so fought across, down the centuries, that what surprises you when you first go there is not their ancientness but their newness. It is not surprising that both are nations deeply, almost mystically, devoted to their land.

In England, according to the landscape historian Christopher Taylor, 'almost every village may have existed by the later eleventh century', but his proviso is important: 'not necessarily with the shape it has now.' The village you see in a classic English landscape painting is not as accidental as it seems. Many of the apparently casual arrangements of houses around a village green and a pond, with the church peeping into the top of the picture, were deliberately planned by landlords. Finchingfield, in Essex, so beloved by Constable-loving calendar-makers and Sunday painters, is just such a deliberate creation. Orderly Finchingfield was clipped on to the older, more irregular settlement. (In the same way, estates of council houses and executive homes have been clipped on to many 'traditional' English villages.)

But, at least, there had generally been a village, of a kind, before the landlord's fiat. Towns, contrariwise, were often planned from scratch, in a medieval fever of land speculation, by abbots, bishops and kings. On the hilltop above Millais's celebrated blind girl, the rainbow vanishes behind the roofs of Winchelsea, in Sussex. This is the classic example of an English planned town that failed; it

is comparable to the *bastide* towns that English kings set down all over south-west France. Half its street grid is empty, and the church was never finished.

You can never escape from the legalism, the middle-class attention to duty, in the English landscape. The only sacred shrine is the law of contract. This faith is embodied in stone or brick. As the early capitalists began to see themselves as men apart, they celebrated their new liberty in privately built churches (as at Salle). They no longer self-effacingly gave money to the local abbot to help him add to his communal establishment. Eventually they would strip the abbot of everything he had, leaving ruins like Fountains or Rievaulx as (to us) a romantic memorial. The extraordinary thing is that so much of these *nouveaux riches'* building work – without which the English landscape of today is unimaginable – took place in a country wracked by the almost endless civil wars of the Middle Ages.

Nothing, of course, is ever so perfect that no one thinks they can improve on it. It was not till the eighteenth century that landlords seriously set about the architectural adornment of the landscape, with the deliberate aim of making it fit their aesthetic preconceptions. The idea of the picturesque triumphed. Often its major achievements were fenced off, like England's largest single work of art, Stowe park. But the proprietorial eye, like the proprietorial writ, went far beyond the fence. Architecture with no purpose other than to be looked at began to besprinkle the landscape: King Alfred's Tower, for example, within sight of Stourhead, or the sham castle at Wimpole. All became, in due course, central to the Romantic topography of men like John Piper or Eric Ravilious. England became the land of follies.

Without this picturesque passion, there would be fewer obelisks and memorials of all kinds in the English landscape. Stoodley Pike is the prime example from my childhood. Another, near Sunderland, is a grandiloquent hilltop pastiche of the Theseum in Athens. Built in honour of 'Radical Jack' Lambton, it looms like an apparition as the clouds come in from the North Sea. In England, a folly was not always pure madness; often it was an architectural emblem. In Cumberland, Charles Howard, eleventh Duke of Norfolk, admired the new-fledged, liberty-loving United States. So he built a farm called Jefferson, near his residence at Greystoke Castle, and another called Fort Putnam. The cowshed at Fort Putnam has a wall with castellations that look like *Alice Through the Looking Glass* chess pieces. Not far away stands the obelisk of Greystoke Pillar. (Tarzan, in his own way a symbol of Liberty, was Lord Greystoke when he was away from the jungle.) The historian of follies, Barbara Jones, thinks that 'the Howards probably come out top of the list of folly-building families'. At Castle Howard, near York, Vanburgh and Hawksmoor helped them adorn the landscape.

After the picturesque, the sublime. It was the growth of industry – often financed by the same landowners who delighted in follies – which shifted the emphasis. Edmund Burke defined the sublime: 'In nature dark, confused, uncertain images have a greater power on the fancy to form the grander passions than those have which are more clear and determinate.' Erasmus Darwin saw the sublime in steam :

The Giant-Power from earth's remotest caves
Lifts with strong arm her dark reluctant waves,
Each caverned rock and hidden den explores,
Drags her dark coals, and digs her shining ores.
Next, in close cells of ribbèd oak confined,
Gale after gale, he crowds the struggling wind;
The imprisoned storms through brazen nostrils roar,
Fan the white flame, and fuse the sparkling ore.
Here high in air the rising stream he pours
To clay-built cisterns or to lead-lined towers;
Fresh through a thousand pipes the wave distils,
And thirsty cities drink the exuberant rill.

The landscape of the Industrial Revolution was Miltonic. To John Martin it was the inspiration for his doom-laden illustrations to *Paradise Lost*. To Turner it supplied steam to put among rain and wind. At Matlock, in Derbyshire, John Smedley manufactured health: he promoted the hydropathic cure. Many years later, the future architectural historian, John Summerson, happened to find himself, as a child, at a school housed in the mansion Smedley built for himself in the 1860s. Riber Castle, long derelict, still rises above the Derbyshire fields, a grotesque, bastard mixture of Gothic and Renaissance styles. Summerson, looking back, asked :

'How could such a building possibly have happened? It still rivets attention in that big-boned Derbyshire landscape; to have lived in it is to have experienced raw, uncouth, sub-architectural qualities not often met with

and, once encountered, not easily forgotten. And there is one memory of Riber which, for me, will always justify its enormities. It belongs, as I remember, to early mornings of late summer or early autumn, when the valley below becomes a giant bowl of mist, of the density and whiteness of cotton wool. The sun comes up behind the castle and projects its shadow on the surface of the mist. Fantastically elongated, the shadow reaches all the way to Matlock Bank, an image of incredible majesty and elegance. As the mist dissolves so does the image and the shelving hydros of Matlock Bank take its place. The spell withdraws into the carcase on Riber Hill.'

But as England began to slip behind the United States and Germany in the international industrial race, everything from the great industrial age moved back from the sublime to the picturesque. The postcard makers of Cornwall judge a deserted tin-mine gear-house and chimney to be as pretty as St Michael's Mount in its bay. In the Dales, at Ribblehead, a many-arched railway viaduct gives aesthetic purpose to a rather desolate spot. It is now scarcely used by trains, but there was an outcry when British Rail proposed to pull it down. (Conservationists are similarly sharpening their oratory to protect the Nato early-warning radomes on Fylingdales Moor, which Reyner Banham hoped might yet become England's first plastic ruin.) Ribblehead viaduct verged on follydom even when it was built. (Later critics may say the same about Fylingdales.) It carried a line driven through in the last great passion for railway construction, when it was assumed that the grander the project, the better it would pay. It didn't.

In England, landscape and architecture have grown together, in symbiosis. Buildings have tended to respect the spirit of the place they are built in. (I would argue that this is even true of the spreading tentacles of suburban semis: under Voysey's influence, they hugged the lie of the land.) There are examples the other way, inevitably. At Kedleston, Robert Adam cleared away village and road, and built a Palladian mansion in Derbyshire, which captured faithfully the traditional coldness and arrogance of the Curzons (motto: 'Let Curzon Holde What Curzon Helde'). The extreme counter-example is Blenheim Palace. It is unique in England. It might be in Bavaria or Spain, with its insistence on dominating, even crushing, the landscape.

The country house was usually, in Professor Hoskins's words, 'a warmth of red brick, a flash of stucco, among luxuriant trees'. The baroque in England was a foreign flower, and not much appreciated, as Abel Evans's epitaph for Vanburgh, the architect of Blenheim, showed:

Lie heavy on him, Earth! for he
Laid many a heavy load on thee!

The English see their landscape as like an apple: they do not want it bruised. Baroque is brutal. Perhaps, too, this is why the English landscape is less severely engineered than that of the United States or most continental states. It may be partly a function of the close-packed population. The first heroic stretch of the M1 was built almost like a railway, in as straight a line as it could be, even through the Dunstable Downs. Owen Williams's brutalist bridges did nothing to relieve its fierceness. But later English motorways have seldom cut a swathe through the countryside in the way *autoroutes* (or the high-speed TGV rail lines) do in France.

Bridges are the high point of architectural engineering. In northern England the passion is little abated since Victorian days. The Brunel of the motorways was the Lancashire roads engineer, James Drake. He interlaced north-west England – from Shap Fell to the Cheshire plain – with more such roads, proportionately, than Los Angeles. For much of his career, his stately job-title was County Surveyor and Bridgemaster. He was perhaps proudest of his bridge over the river Lune. He put a picture of it, with swans in the foreground, into his 1969 monograph on motorways. Across the Humber, the Barton Bridge (itself a commercial folly outdoing Ribblehead) was, in its day, the largest single span in Europe. The north has a bolder view of landscape. In the south of England, nerves have grown weaker. The virtuoso of present-day European bridge-building is the architect-engineer, Santiago Calatrava. He proposed an elegant arc to carry the North Circular Road southwards across the bleak Thames estuary, east of the Royal Docks. His design had nothing of the strange beauty of some of his continental bridges. These can be more like built demonstrations of stress patterns than traditional bridges. But it had a simple elegance, like Sydney Harbour Bridge, or the Golden Gate, bridging the river like a rainbow, and adding

something to a landscape that otherwise lacked any definition. It was rejected.

Only telecommunications have the magic power that railways once had. At Clare, in Constable country, the Victorian railway builders cavalierly cut through the medieval castle mound, to make room for a station yard. That was Progress, and no one complained. So it is now with television masts. Above the Chilterns, at Stokenchurch, the tall Telecom tower is the most visible component of the landscape. It makes a mockery of the elaborate trouble taken to slice the M40 unobtrusively through the escarpment. When it was proposed to reconstruct the west front of Wells Cathedral, a bitter argument broke out; but in the Mendips, high above the cathedral towers, a slender mast announces where real cultural power now lies. At Holmfirth, a tapering concrete turret, like a gigantic lighthouse, soars so tall above the Pennines that you can see it across half of West Yorkshire. This is our contemporary landscape. But painters very rarely include such things in their pictures. As with pylons (in spite of Blomfield), they look the other way. Like mill chimneys, these newcomers will only be accepted when they have outlived their use.

The English painter who, more than any other, celebrated landscape with architecture in it was John Sell Cotman. To him, landscape almost *was* architecture. With Gainsborough, Constable and Crome, he made up that magnificent quartet of East Anglians, who created classic English landscape painting. The fragility of Cotman's water-colours means that he is less known, even now, than the other three. In his life, too, he was blighted by melancholia and a congenital inability to get on in the world. When he died in 1842, not a single obituary was published, even in Norwich, the city of his birth. But in his work, as Joanna Drew wrote, 'we find expressions of experience, of landscape and of architecture, whose gravity and complexity defy their modest scale and sparse simplicity'. (Turner's work is equally unimaginable without architecture. But he played a different game. He dissolved architecture and landscape into a single element: not castles in the air, but castles that *were* air.)

As a young man, Cotman drew and painted the ornaments in the grounds of Castle Howard. He has some affinity with Poussin, and his neo-classicism may derive from eighteenth-century landscape gardening.

When the art critic David Thompson made a television film in 1982, for the bicentenary of Cotman's birth, he went to Greta Bridge, the subject of perhaps Cotman's best-known picture. In an essay written for an Arts Council exhibition that same year, Thompson wrote: 'If there is one contemporary who matches Cotman's unique blend of neo-classic elegance with picturesque incident, it is that idiosyncratic [and, incidentally, Masonic] architect, Sir John Soane. Soane's famous low, elongated arch has as much to do with what Cotman made of Greta Bridge as the actual Greta Bridge did.' The arch of the real bridge, Thompson found, is close to a perfect semi-circle.

Cotman was, at times, a pure topographer. He produced volumes of architectural etchings. This was partly, but not entirely, in the hope of making money to support his family. His painting was imbued with architecture, and its use of space. The remarkable picture called *Chirk Aqueduct* (which may be a transplanted Roman aqueduct, rather than Telford's) conveys the fascination that any great bridge has: a solid structure, part of the landscape, whose whole purpose is movement (of people, vehicles, fluids) across that landscape. To capture this feeling of solidity and change, Cotman combines the precision of pencil and the transparency of water-colour. Again and again in Cotman, the homogeneous blocks of colour resemble an ethereal architecture, as if he saw a new order, even in copses and streams; in the woods of Barnard Castle, for example, or the pool of Hell Cauldron, on the Greta.

Cotman, of course, knew Salle church, and drew it.

BOOK LIST

Sources include:

Reyner Banham, 'On a distant prospect . . .', in Paul Barker (editor), *Arts in Society*, Fontana, 1977.

Alan Bowness and others, *The Pre-Raphaelites*, Tate Gallery and Penguin, 1984.

John Sell Cotman, *Excursions in the County of Norfolk*, Longman, Hurst, Rees, Orme & Brown, 1818.

James Drake, *Motorways*, Faber & Faber, 1969.

Richard A. Fellows, *Sir Reginald Blomfield*, A. Zwemmer, 1985.

Mark Girouard, *Town and Country*, Yale University Press, 1992.

W. G. Hoskins, *The Making of the English Landscape,* Hodder & Stoughton, revised edn, with notes by Christopher Taylor, 1988.

Barbara Jones, *Follies & Grottoes*, Constable, revised edn, 1974.

Francis D. Klingender, *Art and the Industrial Revolution*, Evelyn, Adams & Mackay, revised edn, 1968.

Roger Lonsdale, *The New Oxford Book of Eighteenth Century Verse*. Oxford University Press, 1984.

John Newman and others, *Blickling Hall*, National Trust, 1987.

Nikolaus Pevsner, *The Englishness of English Art,* Penguin, revised edn, 1964.

Nikolaus Pevsner and others, *The Buildings of England*, Penguin, 1951–1992.

Miklos Rajnai and others, *John Sell Cotman, 1782–1842*, Arts Council of Great Britain, 1982.

Dennis Sharp (editor), *Santiago Calatrava*, Book Art, 1992.

James Curl Stevens, *The Art and Architecture of Freemasonry*, Batsford, 1991.

John Summerson, *The Unromantic Castle*, Thames & Hudson, 1990.

John Summerson and others, *John Soane*, Academy Editions, 1983.

Once in the wind of morning
  I ranged the thymy wold;
The world-wide air was azure
  And all the brooks ran gold.

There through the dews beside me
  Behold a youth that trod,
With feathered cap on forehead,
  And poised a golden rod.

With mien to match the morning
  And gay delightful guise
And friendly brows and laughter
  He looked me in the eyes.

Oh whence, I asked, and whither?
  He smiled and would not say,
And looked at me and beckoned
  And laughed and led the way.

And with kind looks and laughter
  And nought to say beside
We two went on together,
  I and my happy guide.

Across the glittering pastures
  And empty upland still
And solitude of shepherds
  High in the folded hill,

By hanging woods and hamlets
  That gaze through orchards down
On many a windmill turning
  And far-discovered town,

With gay regards of promise
  And sure unslackened stride
And smiles and nothing spoken
  Led on my merry guide.

By blowing realms of woodland
  With sunstruck vanes afield
And cloud-led shadows sailing
  About the windy weald,

By valley-guarded granges
  And silver waters wide,
Content at heart I followed
  With my delightful guide.

And like the cloudy shadows
  Across the country blown
We two fare on for ever,
  But not we two alone.

With the great gale we journey
  That breathes from gardens thinned,
Borne in the drift of blossoms
  Whose petals throng the wind;

Buoyed on the heaven-heard whisper
  Of dancing leaflets whirled
From all the woods that autumn
  Bereaves in all the world.

And midst the fluttering legion
  Of all that ever died
I follow, and before us
  Goes the delightful guide,

With lips that brim with laughter
  But never once respond,
And feet that fly on feathers,
  And serpent-circled wand.

A. E. Housman

The future of our past *Margaret Drabble*

Bill Brandt *Willy Lott's Cottage* 1975

No white nor red was ever seen
So amorous as this lovely green.

These lines were written more than a hundred years before the Romantic poets 'discovered' nature, and they foreshadow the extraordinary love affair of the English writer with the English landscape. They are by Andrew Marvell (1621–78), poet and statesman, and they come from one of his most famous poems, *The Garden*, in which he celebrates the delights of solitude and repose, and imagines himself, having exhausted the carnal passions, enjoying more spiritual pleasures:

Annihilating all that's made
To a green thought in a green shade.

The transition from amorousness to greenery is wholly deliberate and highly revealing. Marvell was a fine love poet, but even in his plea *To his Coy Mistress* he finds himself speculating with a hint of longing on 'a vegetable love' that would have time to grow 'vaster than empires, and more slow'. One could argue that the notoriously unamorous English are as much in love with lawns, fountains, waterfalls and vegetables as they ever are with their mistresses.

Those first two lines of Marvell recently caught my eye adorning a poster portraying green fields and a distant castle. It had been issued, as I recall, by the British Tourist Authority, and hung framed upon the wall of a professor of English literature in the Mid-West of the United States. In the late, cold, brown, colourless, muddy spring of Minnesota, it promised escape. It also gave rise to renewed reflections on the nature of British landscape obsession.

The use of that word 'green' is telling. Green is a troubling as well as a soothing colour. The use of green in clothes, paint and décor has always been particularly divisive and controversial. People disagree about greens, except when they occur naturally. They disagree strongly about their representation or imitation in art. Conventions of green in art vary from age to age, and as landscape painting increased in popularity, first Constable, then the Pre-Raphaelites, then Augustus John and J. D. Innes, then Piper and Sutherland (perhaps especially Sutherland) and the Nashes and Ivon Hitchens and

Lanyon and their successors were accused of getting green wrong. They painted too brightly, they made green unnaturally vivid – or, conversely, they painted too murkily and muddily. Brown or greenish brown, which is more natural? To restore, or not to restore?

Is green an erotic colour? Obviously not. Neither, come to that, is brown. That is not the point of them. They speak for nature, and nature (*pace* Erasmus Darwin on *The Loves of the Plants*, and D. H. Lawrence and his lessons on the sex of catkins in *Women in Love*, and Proust on the bee) – nature has been largely thought of by humans as asexual, almost as an escape from sex. This is why the word 'amorous' combines here with 'green' so brilliantly, so disturbingly. Is there something wrong with the British, that they sublimate their sexual instincts in a love of gardens and forests and mountain walks? It is all very well to cultivate a beautiful garden during or after a rich and tumultuous life, as did Vita Sackville-West and Elizabeth Smart, as does Penelope Mortimer, as did Angus Wilson, but is there not something wrong with *substituting* the one for the other?

Wordsworth is a key figure in this debate. The towering eminence of the English Romantic movement, whose influence remains inescapable, he certainly did not write erotic poetry – although recently published letters have revealed an unexpectedly intimate and physically tender relationship with his wife Mary. His passions, in his poetry, were directed towards mountains and lakes, vagrants and shepherds, flowers and trees. Unlike his contemporary Goethe, the comparably influential figure of the German Romantic movement, he did not seek sexual liberation by deserting the cold repressive climes of his youth and catching venereal disease in Rome – a price well worth paying, perhaps, for the *Roman Elegies*. He did, it is true, have a youthful misalliance in revolutionary France which produced an illegitimate daughter, but the oblique poetry he wrote about his love affair (the 'Vaudracour and Julia' episode in Book IX of *The Prelude*) is far inferior to Goethe's love poetry and to his own best work. Byron and Shelley, Romantic poets of the next generation, twitted Wordsworth with being a solemn and unsexual man, and themselves wrote much of their own sexual passion, but by then their austere predecessor had set a signpost which directed a century of English poetry down another lane. English poetry took the green path towards Tennyson, the Georgians, Edward Thomas, Dylan Thomas, R. S. Thomas.

And not only poetry had been redirected. The sensibility of the nation underwent a profound change. Where Wordsworth led, novelists, painters, teachers, preachers, followed. The cult of landscape, now captured in British Tourist Authority posters as well as in contemporary paintings and sculpture, prospered. For many, it replaced other cults. Landscape became sex became religion. A form of pantheism prevailed.

Much has been written in recent years about our changing appreciation of nature and landscape and the process of that change is still at work. I myself wrote a book on the subject, *A Writer's Britain* (1979), in which I tried to trace the way in which writers had altered our vision, popularised certain styles of scenery (Wordsworth and the Lake District; Walter Scott, Robert Burns and Scotland; the Brontes and the Yorkshire Moors; Hardy and Dorset – to quote some obvious examples). I also dealt with the effects on the artistic consciousness of industrialisation, urbanisation and pollution, and the way in which writers attempted to accept or even glorify these invasions into the natural world by treating them as an aspect of the sublime. The text, originally conceived simply as a companion to Jorge Lewinski's photographs of writers' houses, grew and grew. The subject seemed inexhaustible.

Clearly, there was considerable overlap between writers and painters: theorists of the picturesque influenced and were satirised by Jane Austen and Thomas Love Peacock, James Thomson inspired Turner, and that *locus classicus* of the sublime, Gordale Scar near Malham, attracted Thomas Gray and Thomas Girtin, James Ward and John Inchbold, Sir George Beaumont and John Piper, and in their footsteps the lovers in my own novel, *The Waterfall*. (It is to a modern eye a deeply amorous sexual symbol, a female symbol, though pre-Freudian admirers did not consciously see it in those terms.) Much had already been written on art and landscape (with Christopher Hussey on *The Picturesque* (1927), Kenneth Clark on *Landscape into Art* (1949), and John Berger on *Ways of Seeing* (1972), as important landmarks or trail-blazers in the story) but there was far more to come. We learned of low peasant horizons (John Clare), of lofty landowning viewpoints (James Thomson), and began to

reconsider, as the poet Crabbe had done in the eighteenth century, the aesthetic sensibilities of the labourer: the title of John Barrell's *The Dark Side of the Landscape: Rural Poverty 1730–1840* (1980) indicated the direction of much interesting new research. Landscape was a theme that in this country seemed to increase its hold on the scholarly and the creative imagination.

Is there something peculiarly English about the love of landscape? Nikolaus Pevsner thought there was. His Reith Lecture, 'The Englishness of English Art' (1955), ends with a discussion of the importance of the landscape garden, a form which in the mind of its devotees and patrons was associated with notions of political liberty, freedom from constraint, and sympathy with natural organic form. The gardens of Stourhead roused him to unusual heights of rapture: 'In thinking back on the whole of the grounds of Stourhead, and especially the walk round the lake, the reader may agree with the writer that English picturesque landscaping of the eighteenth century is the most beautiful form of gardening ever created . . .' (*Wiltshire*, 1963).

Yet the picturesque garden was not, as we all know, natural. It may have been more natural than Marvell's garden, with its sundial made of herbs and flowers, but it was not as natural as Wordsworth's plot at Dove Cottage, or Mrs Gaskell's preacher-farmer grandfather's kitchen garden at Sandlebridge. Nor was it as natural as John Clare's molehills and ditches and copses, or the Welsh cornfields described by Gerard Manley Hopkins, or Alasdair Maclean's bleak crofts at Ardnamurchan. The picturesque garden was extravagantly expensive and highly artificial, and often involved the removal of vast tracts of earth, the diversion of water from its courses, and, perhaps worst of all (as Cowper lamented), the lopping of ancient avenues of trees. The extensive literature surrounding the subject of landscape gardening and the picturesque is by no means quietist or harmonious in tone. Battles raged and bitter insults were exchanged. The whole subject was highly if on the whole enjoyably contentious.

It remains so. We may still debate whether or not Wordsworth's vision would have been possible without his precursor Thomas Gray, whether Gray would have been able to see as he did without his Claude glass, whether English landscape is often unconsciously seen through a continental filter. (Hanging in a bedroom we have two pleasant unpretentious little prints, side by side. One is of Malvern, the other of Cintra. They are almost identical. From a distance, it is hard to tell which is which, so powerful is the convention that composed them.) Gardening, apparently the most harmless of diversions, is still a divisive topic, a minefield of social snobbery.

Nor is it, as any keen gardener will affirm, a wholly restful and escapist pastime. Gardening is a constant struggle against nature as well as a collaboration with it. It is hard work. It represents our deeply divided feelings about freedom and restraint, wilderness and cultivation. Angus Wilson gave the title *The Wild Garden* (1963, reprinted 1992) to his autobiographical volume on the sources of creative energy, one of the most penetrating accounts of this subject I know: in it he explores his own deep moral and psychological conflicts through the contrasting metaphors of the English 'wild garden' and the pioneer 'garden in the wild', both deeply rooted in his own family history and in the tensions between his pioneering South African mother and his rentier Scottish father. Gardens are not necessarily peaceful. Nature is not necessarily our friend. Eden may have been a garden, but according to Marvell's friend Milton it needed a great deal of management to keep it in order, even before the Fall. And what of the serpent?

We do not have many poisonous serpents in England. We have killed off all the wolves. We do not have poison ivy, or rabid bats. As Aldous Huxley pointed out in his essay *Wordsworth in the Tropics*, maybe this is one of the reasons why the English are so fond of nature. It is, relatively, benign. Is it this mildness that has produced our landscape artists, our landscape poets? Horace Walpole, that great arbiter of taste, offers ambiguous testimony on this point – referring also, with unusual frankness, to the notorious problem of the unmentionable British weather: in a wet June he writes to his cousin 'If I turn to the left, I see my hay soaking under the rain; and on the right I have a good fire – 'tis pity we ever imported from the Continent ideas of summer: nature gave us coal mines in lieu of it, and beautiful verdure, which is inconsistent with it, so that an observation I made forty years ago, is most true, that this country exhibits the most beautiful landscapes in the world when they are framed and glazed, that is, when you look at them through the window.'

This is a worrying statement, for those who like their nature and their paintings to be natural. It reminds one that Walpole acquired many of his discriminating opinions not in wet England but on the European Grand Tour, and that despite England's infatuation with landscape, painters have often felt compelled to escape to brighter light and sunnier scenery. A few continental painters, it is true, have made the return journey – Monet, Sisley, Pissarro, Kokoschka, for example – and some English painters, like Therese Oulton, declare a positive affection for England's poor light. Most of the painterly traffic, however, has been in the other direction.

And the real problem of representation is not really connected with the cold, the dark and the wet of Britain but with the nature of reality itself, and with the changing nature of nature. Are we perhaps in the future condemned to sit by a fire, looking out at a view through a glazed window, or perhaps to bask in our central heating as we gaze at a landscape painting which represents a landscape we can no longer see?

Our attitudes to the natural world, as has been said, are not constant, and distinctively new ways of viewing landscape were beginning to emerge in the 1970s and 1980s, as a different kind of greenness became fashionable. Green politics and green petrol and rainbow-coloured warriors entered our consciousness and our language, and Greenery began to be exploited by commercial interests. Serious scholars were also at work. One of the pioneers in this field, W. G. Hoskins, was succeeded by many writers whose interest in the history of place was more ecological than antiquarian: Richard Mabey and Oliver Rackham are among those who opened our eyes both to the fragility and to the enduring recuperative powers of nature, and who extended our awareness of its transformations through history.

While they have tended to dwell on man's long co-operation with nature, some artists have sought the wilderness, and have taken at times a strangely non-interventionist position. They do not look through glazed windows: they work outdoors, use natural materials, and show a marked – some would say excessive – respect for the environment. Andy Goldsworthy makes giant snow balls and stitches leaves; Richard Long and Hamish Fulton walk, as Coleridge walked. In principle they reject the technological world. We can no longer feel today the innocent enthusiasm that those two dissimilar writers Virginia Woolf and Rudyard Kipling both felt for the motor car in its early days, as they bowled enraptured through the fields and downs and woods of Sussex. We cannot guiltlessly enjoy the aerial view from aeroplane or helicopter. We are too ecological for that. Our flights destroy. They destroy us and our planet. Saul Bellow was right to point out that man's new ability to see the clouds from above may have had a deep effect on the human psyche, but a generation later we see the dangers of this vision as well as its possibilities.

Poets also continue to work intensely, almost obsessively, with scenes from a rural rather than a post-industrial and technologically advanced world. An extensive survey of poems published in the early 1990s showed a high proportion dealing with such traditional 'poetic' subjects as landscapes and seascapes, gardens and islands, village life and wildernesses: an interesting subsection (for example, Paul Muldoon's *Madoc*, closely based on readings of Wordsworth, Coleridge and Southey) concerned itself with pioneer explorations of virgin territory, with maps and historical accounts of invasions of the wild. For one poem set on the football terraces we find two about picking blackberries and three about the skulls of birds or animals. Skulls and skeletons and the processes of decay prove a particularly popular theme, recalling Hamish Fulton's unease at the thought of a badger's skull being exposed as an *objet trouvé* in a Manhattan gallery, his anxiety about interfering with a green stain from a pot plant that had dripped on to a work prepared and ready to be sent to the framer. Has not the green stain its own green rights?

On the darker side of the landscape, the poetry survey also revealed several interesting meditations on the nasty things that lie buried beneath the earth's crust, waiting to bubble up. Methane gas or radon accumulates, tips and rubbish dumps fester, and their effluence reaches and inspires the writer and the painter. A recently exhibited work by Maurice Cockrill called *Landfill* has a dangerous, vital glowing beauty. Hell burns beneath us. Is this the new subterranean sublime? A hole in the ground, these days, I am told, is worth more as a hole than the gravel that is quarried from it. This is a startling concept: the price we set on the void.

Inevitably, we must speculate that this widespread

artistic and social interest in rural landscape and the forces that threaten it reflects a deep if at times subconscious anxiety about our future and the future of the planet. Climatologists thunder their ecological warnings at us daily, with conflicting messages, and according to our temperaments we respond with optimism, with cynicism, with fatalism. Or we retreat to a rural corner where we do not read the paper or watch the screen. There are still such corners, even in overpopulated Britain, and writers and artists tend to seek them out – but even there, perhaps, methane bubbles up from its hidden cauldrons.

It can be no coincidence, as we often cautiously suggest, that the Romantic movement was born in the late eighteenth century, as the Industrial Revolution began to gather momentum, as rural England smelled danger, as cottage industries began to give way to factories. We learn to love, too late, what is already vanishing, and seek what has already passed away.

There is an inevitability about this that is beyond reproach and regret. If we accept (as I do) that our early years form our artistic sensibilities and creative conflicts, then of course we must also accept that everything falls and vanishes from us as we grow older. We strive to make sense of the past, but even if we succeed we are dying as we achieve that success. As the novelist Angela Carter said shortly before her untimely death, in some mysterious way as we grow older our past becomes our future. The hand of joy, as Keats, who died even more prematurely, too keenly perceived, is ever at his lips, bidding adieu. Art is an attempt to recapture that which we know must disappear. The historical vision of Hoskins, Mabey and Rackham (like, perhaps, the vision of Freud, so oddly foreshadowed in the thesis of Wordsworth's *Prelude*), helps us to prolong our past and seek in it our future.

One of the reasons why we love landscape, and find it consoling, is because it changes and decays and yet is renewed. Its life is longer than ours. We believe, with the romantic optimist Shelley, that the earth will, 'like a snake, renew her winter weeds outworn'. Few of us believe these days that we ourselves will be renewed and reborn. We will not climb out of our Stanley Spencer graves. But we believe nature will outlast us.

Or do we? Maybe a new factor has entered – or re-entered – our time consciousness. It is not the Day of

Judgement or Armageddon that we now fear, but the death of the planet. A mortality echoing our own has entered the seasons, the weather, the earth itself. Chaos and turbulence are our new hopes. If all is in flux, maybe we may yet be saved.

And yet, amidst this turbulence, amidst these anxieties and uncertainties, a very strong positive feeling for the history and permanence of the natural world persists, and is expressed both by writers and by painters. Like the English language itself, the landscapes we know change, but they stubbornly survive and remain somehow recognisable. In the past decade, two somewhat surprising and resonant novels appeared, both of which were set in a deeply English rural world, light years from the world of Martin Amis's ironically named *London Fields* (1989). One, *The Remains of the Day* (1989), by the Japanese-born British author Kazuo Ishiguro, deals with country house life in England between the wars and in the 1950s, and, simultaneously, with the nature of Englishness. The other, *The Enigma of Arrival* (1987), by the Trinidad-born V. S. Naipaul, deals in part with the decay of country house life in the 1970s and 1980s. It too is about being, or becoming, part of England. Both bear witness to the extraordinary durability of certain visions of English life and landscape. Both evoke the ancient places of Britain – Salisbury, Stonehenge, a prehistoric Wiltshire. Both are written by writers who might have been expected to reject ancient places and Ishiguro and Naipaul in fact stand out against a generation of non-British-born post-colonial writers infuriated by having been brought up on an inappropriate diet of English rural poetry – Wordsworth's *The Daffodils* has come in for particular abuse, and no academic discussion of post-colonial or 'New' literature now is complete without what has become known as a session of 'daffodil bashing'. (See Jamaica Kinkaid's eponymous heroine Lucy (1991), an Antiguan transplanted to America, who says that she literally wants to destroy all the daffodils she sees, so deep is her loathing of her colonial education and cultural heritage.) Naipaul and Ishiguro, in contrast, maintain that the daffodil is not guilty. In different ways, they celebrate Englishness. Ishiguro evokes a world of lawns and formal gardens, of silver cutlery and old-fashioned manners and motor cars, of stunted emotions and unexpressed tenderness and devious behaviour – a vanished world,

which yet lingers on. It is a world which does not understand itself and maybe never did. Naipaul's largely autobiographical novel, in contrast, is about the process of self-recognition, about becoming, about seeing not only England but oneself in England.

It is an extraordinarily evocative account of what can fairly be described as a kind of love affair and marriage with rural England. The first section, 'Jack's Garden', describes the narrator's reactions on his first arrival in England to rain, snow, cold, wet, the seasons; to the incomprehensible London of Earl's Court; and to the ancient landscapes of Wiltshire, where he eventually rents a house on an old decaying estate. These landscapes are not idealised: the narrator acutely observes the untidy jumble of black plastic sacks and old farm vehicles and corrugated iron and barbed wire that make up the countryside today. But nevertheless the father-in-law of his neighbour Jack (glimpsed carrying a load of sticks) reminds the narrator of Wordsworth's leech gatherer, for he cannot choose but see the landscape through the lenses of literature and art. Constable and Augustus John and E. H. Shepherd are also invoked, and Naipaul's meditations on the haunting phrase 'water meadow' remind one of that honorary Englishman Henry James's affection for what seemed to him the quintessentially English and beautiful phrase, 'summer afternoon'.

There is something here that will not die, though decay is one of the themes of the novel, as it is of Ishiguro's. Naipaul paints the dwindling of a great estate – which in real life belonged to the aesthete Stephen Tennant: once sixteen gardeners had worked where now there was only one. Once Stephen Tennant was the most beautiful young man in Britain: now he is old and ill and raddled and fat. (Naipaul has also changed the names of Stephen Tennant's housekeepers in his fictional version: in real or rather in somewhat unreal life, as Philip Hoare's recent biography reveals, they were, wonderfully, called Mr and Mrs Skull.)

Midway through the book, in a section called 'Ivy', Naipaul describes a small epiphany of arrival. He has been ill after a long and difficult journalistic assignment abroad, and as he convalesces in his rented home as spring arrives he observes the peony

. . . pushing up tight, swelling buds on rhubarb-like stalks below the sitting-room window of my cottage.

In my twenty years on and off in England I must have seen many thousands of peonies. They were a common flower, as I was to see when I was fit enough to take bus rides into Salisbury. Right through the valley, in open, sun-struck gardens, I saw them blooming away too fast in bright light, losing their tightness and deep colour, rapidly losing their virtue. None of the many thousand I had seen before this spring had made an impression on me; I had never been able to put the name 'peony' to any of them; I had never been able to attach them to a season or a time of year or to the appearance of other flowers or natural events. These peonies of my convalescence, these peonies around my cottage, were my first; and they stood for my new life.

One would not wish to be narrowly patriotic or chauvinistic about this vision of England. One of the traditional virtues of the English – or of the British, as perhaps we should call ourselves – has been their tolerance, as Pevsner remarked. In their better moments the British have welcomed refugees, like Pevsner himself, and they have learned from and absorbed and been revitalised by traditions from America and the Continent and an ever widening world. The British novel has gained greatly from Henry James, Naipaul, Ishiguro, Salman Rushdie: in the same way poetry has gained from Sylvia Plath and Seamus Heaney and many other borderers and visitors. And a vision of the English landscape is not something that can be exclusively possessed. It is beyond nationalism and ownership.

Wordsworth himself, in his fine sonnet to the imprisoned Haitian hero, Toussaint L'Ouverture (which perhaps should replace *The Daffodils* in text books for overseas students), proclaimed the international communion of man and nature in words that deliberately transcend all national frontiers:

Live, and take comfort. Thou hast left behind
Powers that will work for thee; air, earth, skies;
There's not a breathing of the common wind
That will forget thee; thou hast great allies;
Thy friends are exultations, agonies,
And love, and man's unconquerable mind.

Wordsworth believed that air, earth and skies worked for freedom. For him this was not a metaphor, although landscape metaphor is so deeply rooted in the English language that we hardly notice it. He believed it was so. And that belief in the good powers of the natural world has not yet abandoned us.

Personally I'd like to lose myself in nature, grow again *with* nature, *like* nature, have the stubborn shades of the rocks, the rational obstinacy of the mountain, the fluidity of the air, and the warmth of the sun. In a green my whole brain would flow in unison with the sap rising through a tree's veins. Out in front of us there is a vast presence of light and love, the hovering universe, the tentativeness of things.

Paul Cézanne

I paint the weather and high places and the places where solids and fluids meet. The junction of sea and cliff, wind and cliff, the human body and places all contribute to this concern.

Peter Lanyon

Landscape as experience and as vision   *Norbert Lynton*

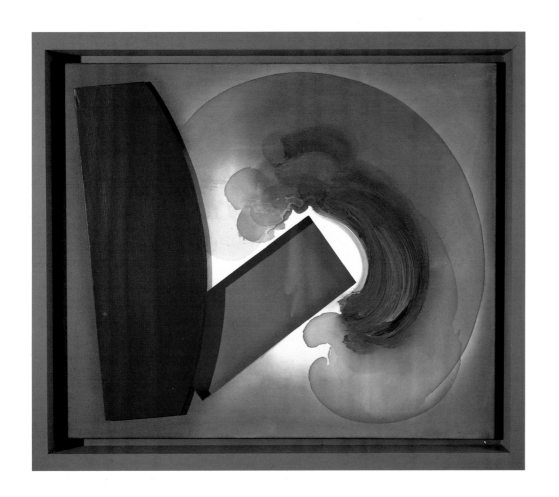

William Tillyer *Horcum* 1993

I was in my teens when I stood in Bedford Square and was struck by the shocking fact that London is built on earth. Those trees and that patch of green stuff in the middle were and are not a large saucerful of nature brought into London but nature, London's bed and base, allowed to peep through the paving slabs and kerbstones, the hard road surfaces and buildings set shoulder to shoulder. Of course, in a way I knew that some houses have gardens and some streets and squares have trees, and that there are parks large enough to prove nature's presence. But these seemed to be licensed intrusions rather than vestigial oases in a world of waterproof surfaces and drains. The urban environment ruled my perceptions. Born in one capital city, I had been raised in another. I admit I could not have starred in Betty Smith's best-selling novel *A Tree Grows in Brooklyn* (1943) – in which (if memory serves) a little girl wins first prize in an essay-writing competition on the subject of trees, by sending in one sentence: 'I cannot write anything about trees because I have never seen one.' (Elia Kazan made a highly regarded film out of it in 1945.) I had been taken into semi-natural woodland not far from home as a child, I had nearly drowned in a large lake, I had been given a place in a boarding school between Berkshire towns and had strolled and run in the countryside surrounding it. Yet the city was, and remains, my natural habitat. Is landscape art in all its many forms, the creation of outsiders like myself? What sorts of relationship with nature does it demand and what comes from them?

It matters in many ways. To me a very obvious one is the moral tax demanded from the city dweller. It may be sweet for one who has been long in city pent to look into the fair and open face of nature, but the price is admission of something close to guilt. The city dweller is made to feel incomplete. Virtue, health, jocund sex are the birthright of every country boy and girl, smelling of manure and milk; *our* reward is high culture if we are very lucky, more likely Gin Lane and the pox. Until Romanticism it was possible to see cities as centres of civilisation, even allowing for their concentrated pollution and vice. Yet from ancient times forward everyone has known that there is a better, truer life to be led away from urban hubbub. This truth has been around for so long it must have been recognised when humankind first conurbated enough to become conscious of separation from another kind of world. Long after, the nineteenth century invented the hard, the exclusive, city. Even the parks provided in them seem merely to demonstrate the cities' power to take over the world – and the power of the middle classes to take over gentry properties. Blake knew the regions where the Muses 'wander fair'; they were not urban. Virgil too. The swelling cities made these regions remote and unlikely dreams rather than accessible alternatives.

But why do we pay this tax? Who demands it? It is the modern world's form of original sin, the price of our loss of innocence and exclusion from the Garden. From bliss to toil. We go to nature, to beauty spots and to nature's most expressive performances – sunsets, waterfalls, mountain peaks, dense woodlands – in hopes of a brief glimpse through that archway out of which the angel with the sword drove our first parents, a glimpse of the Heaven that lay about the infancy of the human race. The question is partly whether the arts are to blame for this foolishness. Toiling in our myriad, selfsame, mostly material ways, spurred on by thoughts of gain and the deadening thrills of competition, we ask the arts to direct our feelings and of course we try to direct the arts by letting them know where we like our attentions to be held. Great art responds by shifting the ground under our feet.

Before Romanticism, it is said usefully even though too glibly, nature needed idealising to be apt matter for the arts. Bodies had to be regularised in classical terms. Landscape was the face of nature but a face marred by birthmarks and excrescences that taste shunned. Mountains were obstacles and places of danger, though useful as the habitat of goats and the source of streams; the seas were dangerous too but serviceable to transport for trade and aggression. Land was either useful, life-supporting and looking like it, or not.

The sublime is spoken of as a key invention in that it defined, recognised and justified another dimension of human sensibility to nature. It managed a positive, even a superior, reading of nature's refusal to conform to the classical sense of order, and thus challenged classical values irreparably. But perhaps it was no more than a hype. Launched by Edmund Burke in 1756, the notion of the sublime was picked up with an avidity that should make us suspicious – a new taste thrill for jaded palates, a quickly thrown-up bridge linking 'civilised' humanity to unreformed nature. It secured another generation's interest in the natural environment by adding to the progression of garden images we are taught as an inevitable sequence: from patterned terraces to regular avenues and pools, to the cunning show of cleaned-up natural forms and classical references of the landscape garden, to the wilder theatre of the picturesque gardens and the picturesque taste for less-touched nature (with a suggestion of moral superiority because nature is here less homogenised and more herself) and thus to the grand finales of cataclysmic Alps and raging oceans, with or without hell and damnation. Beyond that, and already hinted at, lies cosmic exploration in fantasy and fact. The self-conscious human race shrank itself to become suppliant before the face of nature as long before it had been suppliant to a vengeful god, and then, nothing if not human, blew itself up again to take imaginary possession of what it worships. Thus we are made whole. We live the urban life, blind to day as to season, and long to submit to nature's influence. We dedicate our lives to toil, but in our imaginations and by means of the artificial breaks that allow us a brief escape from routines of work, we taste paradise. Our deep joy at that – or at least the deadening of pain it brings – signals our wholeness: we have atoned, we are alien no longer, we are at one again in the arms of the good mother who bore us all. Nature is always female.

Artists prepare for us these escapes and excursions as surely as the makers of shoes and yachts, but is that all they do? Which side of the archway do they stand? Romanticism and the Industrial Revolution armed us with hyperbole and polarisation, and we still steer by them. The seventeenth-century painters who provided Dutch burghers with landscapes and seascapes by the cartload were no more and no less detached from their subject-matter than were their clients. Even Amsterdam, densely urban already then, was merely a walk away from open land though much of that was flat and artificial, and no more than a generation or two away from peasant existence. Humanity was in some command of those imaged scenes, even the wilder seascapes. The merchant buying them was honouring and colonising the family's recent past as much as complementing his present situation. The artists too were townsfolk with some roots

still in the land; nature's world was close. By 1800 nature is no part of any artist's nature – with rare exceptions.

Turner was born over his father's barber shop in Covent Garden. His father was 'a chatty old fellow' as his profession required, uneducated but keen to see his son rise. His mother, daughter of a prosperous butcher of Islington, had an 'ungovernable temper' which drew her into insanity. Turner avoided all mention of her. Both of Constable's parents were alive when he died at sixty-one. His father was a well established miller who married the daughter of a well established cooper of London and brought her back to East Bergholt, a village set in fine cultivated and grazed-over country, with many rivers, bridges and houses, trees framing views of church towers and glimpses of the inland sea of the Stour estuary – an environment as much man's as nature's but fashioned symbiotically and one in which neither need feel a stranger. 'The sound of water escaping from Mill dams . . . Willows, Old rotten Banks, slimy posts, & brickwork. I love such things . . .' I am struck by how this well-known quotation from one of Constable's letters to his friend John Fisher refers to things that are nature's and man's and sees them as one.

Turner and Constable sat together at the 1813 Royal Academy banquet, aged thirty-eight and thirty-seven. Constable afterwards spoke of Turner's 'wonderful range of mind'. It truly was an amazing mind, the more so for being home-made and built on rocky foundations. But what impressed Constable so much that evening? What did they speak about? One suspects it was Turner talking and Constable listening, but was there anything Turner could have told Constable about nature and how to paint her? Any two good, serious painters have a lot in common, and I must guard against setting colleagues against each other. Yet in some respects they were opposites: their minds, including their sense of God, their backgrounds and breeding, their social behaviour and the purposes of their art.

Turner had already been a full member of the Royal Academy for more than a decade, a renowned and controversial landscape painter and illustrator who had worked all over England, Scotland and Wales, had built himself a house at Twickenham, owned a suburban one at Hammersmith and rented rooms in Harley Street, and was waiting for the war against Napoleon to end to take up again his visual conquest of western Europe in order to prove himself the greatest landscape painter of all time. Constable was not yet an associate of the Academy, had scarcely travelled outside Suffolk where he still lived when he was not at his London lodgings (in 1820 he settled in the village of Hampstead) and had hardly been noticed by art journalism but was getting some praise from fellow artists. Undoubtedly he had his ambitions too. These included reputation and reward, some recognition of the knowledge as well as the feeling that went into his work, and permission at long last to marry the one woman he ever loved, Maria Bicknell. His art ambition was the modest and outrageous one of painting nature truthfully. That meant learning from his best predecessors, Gainsborough and the Dutch mainly, but then also driving deeper into nature than they or anyone had done. The impulse was pious and regional – patriotic – 'those scenes made me a painter, and I am grateful' – but also scientific and thus once again modern. There was 'the truth at second hand' to be had from pictures, and there was nature to be understood as much as seen, and drawn and painted on the spot. This research would provide a basis of knowledge for exhibitable paintings more often than supply material directly to them. The two categories were quite distinct, investigation and art, though both were in the service of God.

What or whom Turner served is far less clear. With him one turns reluctantly to the modern cliché of an artist working because he had to, creating a world of poetic expression to answer some deep need in himself, allay some deep pain, make a positive act out of a wholly pessimistic view of life – none of which had anything to do with success in art yet led him to pursue that path. More than a model, nature was his victim, just as Europe was Napoleon's, and art was his weapon just as warfare was Napoleon's art. The remarkable fact is that Turner transcended his own programme in a way he cannot have foreseen. In his later work art becomes the thing itself, not a means, let alone a weapon of conquest, but the unknown goal he had been pursuing all the time via all sorts of painterly skills, acute observation of art (including his own work) and of nature, and over-the-top dramatics on behalf of scenery that did not need them (or so it seems to us, after the event). Turner's vast talent was commensurate with his need to learn and then to

unlearn. It is not said often enough that Turner at times showed himself the most vulgar painter the world has known – so blatantly that one is tempted to offer it as evidence of greatness (as for Courbet, but in his case on a narrower scale from excellence to banality). Lawrence Gowing brought his examination of Turner's process of isolating the pictorial effect 'as one skims the cream of milk' to this conclusion: 'He had isolated an intrinsic quality of painting and revealed that it could be self-sufficient, an independent imaginative function.' Painting nature with his persistence, energy and growing wisdom led Turner into painting painting, into making paintings that exploit what nature taught him in the way of colour and tone, energy, composition and texture for their own sake, so that now he was working without his tutor in a world of joy his pessimism had previously closed to him. At times one feels that nature has similarly tutored composers – Delius may be an instance – whilst others it has merely enriched, extending their reach and means.

Constable knew he 'should paint his own places best' and let everyone know that these were his very own world, his childhood, his primitive experience. His possessiveness was centripetal rather than imperial: 'I have a kingdom of my own both fertile and populous – my landscape and my children', he wrote to his friend Fisher in 1823. That was the year in which he rented a house inside London, in Charlotte Street, with a room large enough to paint his 'six-footers', while keeping his place in Hampstead too and often going back to Bergholt. He was beginning to show his large paintings at the Academy, a bold move to catch attention and insist on the intellectual seriousness of his art. Where Turner raised the status of his landscapes by stuffing them with history-type material (Aeneas and the Sybil, Nebuchadnezzar, Hannibal), Constable took the history format and composed and recomposed his pictures for it on the basis of studies and full-size 'sketch' versions. He did not inject into them literary or historical references to associate them with history painting but tuned them to his version of grandiloquence, with much moving of stage props about, enlarging this, reducing that – omitting two children and exchanging the cow on the bridge for a female figure in the case of *View on the Stour*, near Dedham, shown at the Royal Academy in 1822 and bought by the Paris dealer Arrowsmith in 1824. Was he denying the superior truth of direct experience of God's creation or recognising mankind's interference with it?

His world was changing gradually in appearance and quite drastically in spirit. What we call the farming industry declined sharply after 1815 and its weaker members lost their livelihood and way of life. Bankruptcies, unemployment, distant and impersonal management where there had been a close society, riots, poverty, a large part of the rural population uprooted into towns and industrial labour. As Constable learned to manipulate his natural scenes to make them subjects for elevated art, he also learned to make present observation accommodate memories of better times. His earlier art almost persuades us that he was in touch with a Golden Age not yet gone, that some glimpse of it was available to him in his intimacy with the world he was born into. Now the Gates of Paradise close even for him. His reputation and sales are rising. The death of his father-in-law in 1828 brought him a substantial inheritance but Maria died the same year, leaving him bereft with seven children. In 1829 he was made an RA at last, yet it was in 1830 he had the painful experience of hearing one of his smaller landscapes, of water-meadows near Salisbury, condemned as 'a poor thing' and 'very green' by his colleagues on the exhibition committee; as an Academician he had the right to exhibit as he wished, and the picture should not have come up for selection. He refused to let it be hung after hearing it rubbished by his colleagues.

His publication of a set of mezzotints and a text under the title *English Landscape* in 1830–32, feels like a riposte. The prints were worked to bring out the role of light in delivering the abrupt changes and subtler modulations the English climate brings to scenery. As he developed his more artificial paintings, he gave extra time to making those close studies of boats, plants and birds, trees and clouds, in pencil, water-colour or oil that are his most popular works today but were then unexhibitable. In a text to go with his prints he now insisted on the role of this kind of intense observation of nature, as opposed to imitation of others' paintings, as giving access to the 'PRIMITIVE SOURCE, NATURE' and thus also the means of bringing into art 'qualities of Nature unknown to it before'. He recognised that only a few would ever be able to 'appreciate any deviation from a beaten track' or

respond to 'an original cast of mind' or 'consequent novelty of style', and indeed *English Landscape* sold very badly. Constable's pessimism deepened and despair and nostalgia show ever more strongly in his work. He lectured in several places during 1833–36 to prove landscape's place in art, even its place next to history painting as a 'powerful auxiliary'. He died in London on the last day of March 1837 without having convinced the world.

Ruskin treated his art with disdain. Long before Ruskin even the more receptive critics had used Turner's example as a way of highlighting Constable's limitations. As one of them wrote in 1819, after commenting on the vividness of his scenes: 'He does not give a sentiment, a soul, to the exterior of nature as Mr Turner does; he does not at all exalt the spectator's mind . . . but he gives her outward look, her complexion and physical countenance with more exactness. He has none of the poetry of Nature like Mr Turner, but he has more of her portraiture.' When Constable was poetic no one noticed, nor did anyone point out that many of his landscapes sound a note of quiet pleasure that then countered decades of melancholy nature poetry. Ruskin, who in his fifties became obsessed by a 'plague-wind' no one else had noticed, the 'wind of darkness . . . a malignant *quality* of wind coming from the south west', and by the 'plague-cloud', that together '*blanch* the sun instead of reddening it', never noticed that Constable in his late work was beset with a similar vision of bleakness. Perhaps Ruskin never saw Constable's *Hadleigh Castle*, his last great painting, completed in 1829, long after he had visited the scene and made studies of it. Here contentment yields to a gloom close to panic. Ruskin linked the light-quenching sky to 'poisonous smoke' – 'there are at least two hundred furnace chimneys in a square of two miles on every side of me' – and to 'dead men's souls – such of them as are not gone yet where they have to go, and may be flitting hither and thither, doubting, themselves, of the fittest place for them.' Constable's bitter tone we associate with the death of Maria and possibly that and nothing more general is what he referred to in a letter to his brother a month after she died: 'the face of the World is totally changed to me'.

In almost the last of the many pages of *Modern Painters*, Ruskin compares the worlds into which Giorgione and

Turner were born, the vividness of sixteenth-century Venice and the visual and moral ugliness of Covent Garden and Billingsgate absorbed by Turner as a child, then the glories of the Yorkshire hills discovered by the young man, but signs of urban decline everywhere ('in the present work of men, meanness, aimlessness, unsightliness . . . booths of a darksome Vanity Fair, busily base'), and then Europe and Turner's consciousness of war 'on all the hills and plains of the Christian earth, from Moscow to Gibraltar' and 'those bloodstains on the Alpine snow'. Turner's vision, he concluded, was marked from the first by mankind's rottenness and clutter. Turner's mind he saw as of the highest, 'a combination of the minds of Keats and Dante'. It joined 'capricious waywardness' to 'infinite tenderness' and was 'very tolerant of vulgarity, even fond of it in some forms'.

It was this Turner whom Ruskin had chosen for his hero. Both were Londoners; unregulated nature was the other world for them. The great writer chose the great painter as the monument around which to construct a philosophy of art, and of art and society, that makes remarkably little contact with the painter's best art. Constable's piety and loving observation could surely have served Ruskin better. It cannot have been Turner's social graces or compelling discourse that hooked Ruskin's evolving mind to him. In 1836, when he first wrote about Turner's art, defending it against charges of being 'perfectly childish' and flying 'off into mere eccentricities', it was his imagination he praised in the highest terms as 'Shakespearian in its mightiness'. And then he added his appreciation of Turner's sometimes hyperdelicate ways: 'Many coloured mists are floating above the distant city [in *Rome from Mount Avertine*], but such mists as you might imagine to be aetherial spirits, souls of the mighty dead breathed out of the tombs of Italy into the blue of her bright heaven, and wandering in vague and infinite glory around the heaven they have loved', etc. Was Ruskin captivated by Turner's combination of tender poetic powers with a macho reputation, and by whatever sexual implications there might have been in that for the ever-virginal writer? Later it was Turner's truth, his knowledge of rocks, water, plants and air, that got more of Ruskin's attention, while the increasingly broad, almost subjectless paintings of Turner's later years he set aside as the productions of a

deteriorating mind. In consequence neither Turner, successful in spite of his many obscurities, nor Constable who just began to taste success before his world collapsed around him, was seen for what he really was. Turner's due recognition as one of the nineteenth century's greatest painters has been the work of the last thirty years. As for Constable, his art remains what the Redgraves in mid-Victorian times said it was, 'purely and thoroughly English'. He never left this island, mentally any more than physically. That focus was a great strength to him but it effected a narrowing of English art.

Had Turner and Constable been close friends and confidants, collaborators even, there might be more security in linking their names to those of Wordsworth and Coleridge. Wordsworth was Coleridge's senior by two years; Constable was Turner's junior by one. The poets were born about five years before the painters. Turner was his own poet, and a dull one. Constable, whose career touches Wordsworth's at a few points, had a special love for James Thomson's *The Seasons* with its talk of 'guilty cities' as against 'the life / Led by primeval ages uncorrupt' still to be met in the countryside. But his language smacks of the Augustans and contrasts with Wordsworth's primitivism of language and often theme. Wordsworth's quick love for Coleridge once they met in 1797, and his admiration for Coleridge's intellectual agility, is matched by Coleridge's reverence for Wordsworth as the firmly rooted, much more limited thinker, taciturn where Coleridge was brilliantly garrulous, English where Coleridge was European. Richard Holmes sums them up with these words: 'Coleridge was a huge river; while Wordsworth was a mighty rock'.

Coleridge was a man of towns, though born in Devon. His years of schooling were passed in London and Cambridge, and then England's second largest city, Bristol, was his home – if anywhere could be counted the home of this restless man. Wordsworth was born in Cumberland and spent most of his life in Dorset and the Lake District. He pitied his friend for his 'deprived childhood, "in city pent",' as Margaret Drabble writes. Wordsworth knew that cities make men false, and even Coleridge's overwhelming 'learning, gorgeous eloquence . . . subtle speculations, toils abstruse / Among the Schoolmen' he judged

The self-created sustenance of a mind
Debarr'd from Nature's living images,
Compell'd to be a life unto itself,
And unrelentingly possess'd by thirst
Of greatness, love, and beauty.

Had they met sooner, Wordsworth speculated, his 'calmer habits, and more steady voice' could have dispelled the 'airy wretchedness' that was his friend's lot.

Coleridge had literally been deprived, debarred. He was born in the little market town of Ottery St Mary, the youngest of the Reverend John Coleridge's ten children. When John died, before young Sam's ninth birthday, his mother promptly despatched the boy to her brother in London. Coleridge always knew this as his exile, and for the rest of his days sought both his rural roots and a mother's embrace. When he became a father, in 1796, he promised himself that his children would 'be bred up from earliest infancy in the simplicity of peasants, their food, dress and habits completely rustic'. And he launched himself into rustic solitude with a vigour that worried his friends. He reassured one of them: 'I shall have six companions – my Sara (his wife), my Babe, my own shaping and disquisitive Mind, my Books, my beloved Friend Thomas Poole, & lastly, Nature, looking at me with a thousand looks of Beauty, and speaking to me in a thousand melodies of Love.' Discovering William and Dorothy Wordsworth near by the following year felt like completion, yet he still lacked some strong and centering force: 'My mind feels as if it ached to behold & know something great – something *one* & *indivisible* – and it is only in the faith of this that rocks and waterfalls, mountains or caverns give me the sense of sublimity or majesty!'

Wordsworth, wrote A. N. Whitehead, was drunk with nature, a peasant to be sure, a genius who was also 'sane even to the point of prosiness'. The ageing Ruskin described Wordsworth as a peasant too, 'simply a Westmoreland peasant', and could earlier be shrewdly critical of the poet's self-importance ('He has also a vague notion that Nature would not be able to get on well without Wordsworth'). But whereas he loved Coleridge's poetry and credits him with more imagination than Wordsworth could muster, he had no doubt that Wordsworth was 'the greater *man* . . . who may be trusted in everything', his mind 'divinely pure in its

conceptions of pleasure, majestic in the equanimity of its benevolence – intense as white fire with chastised feelings'. Coleridge bold, undisciplined, 'a benevolent man in a fever'; Wordsworth 'grand, consistent, perfectly disciplined'. Ruskin's commitment to Wordsworth's poetry is patent, yet the conflict hinted at here illuminates his conception of Turner as the painter who, until his late decline, 'may be trusted in everything'. Coleridge grips his attention and his heart with boldness and extravagance; Wordsworth he honours as the poet who understood nature deeply, was fair to everyone and everything, and could even find his heart leaping up at the sight of early-morning London before smoke dims the sky and greed kicks the city machine into motion. Coleridge = energy; Wordsworth = judgement. The private Ruskin is pulling one way, the public, didactic one another, though I would generally have thought Ruskin's eloquent parading of many hearts on his sleeve the reason why his writing still fires us. Again, Constable's judgement would seem the better base, and Turner's energy its untrustworthy, seductive opposite. Or was Ruskin so much of an artist that he knew the greater, deeper judgement that is the child of energy – Blake's 'the road of excess' that 'leads to the palace of wisdom'? One notices Ruskin's repeated attempts to come to terms with the poetry of Byron, which obviously he could not approve of, yet, just as obviously, found himself deeply stirred by. He finds in Byron, 'lame demon as he was', a bitterness, a gloom, and 'a sense of the material beauty', remarkable for the 'iridescence, colour-depth and morbid (I use the word deliberately) mystery and softness of it', and then says this 'is found, to the full, only in five men that I know of in modern times: namely, [Jean-Jacques] Rousseau, Shelley, Byron, Turner and myself'. Again, this is the old Ruskin speaking. The middle-aged one has meanwhile been encouraging men younger than himself to adopt the 'clear-struck beauty of Angelico and the Trecentisti'.

If we take Ruskin as a whole we have to acknowledge that he was literally inconclusive: he had many messages to give the world, but not one message. Perhaps his life was not short enough for one message to be saved from it, and perhaps that is his essential gift to Proust. Search is not a straight line and calls for re-search, *recherche*. Proust remembering and writing for endless hours in his cork-lined bedroom; Ruskin bent over many a desk or table, mind and ink meeting in his not over neat but fine and intelligent handwriting, mile upon mile over acres upon acres of paper ('for you know he is intensely occupied and never with us but at meal times', his wife Effie reported from Venice to her mother); Wordsworth walking, finding and constructing his poems as he walked, building moments of perception into monuments of considered experience, the creations of what he called a 'feeling intellect' and, earlier, 'passion, which itself / Is highest reason in a soul sublime.' De Quincey calculated that Wordsworth 'must have traversed a distance of 175,000 to 180,000 English miles' in his long working life. And suddenly we understand why Constable does not quite measure up to Wordsworth and why Ruskin needed Turner. They were all tireless workers, but there just was not enough of Constable. Dying at sixty-one after a slow start, he had not done enough. Turner died at seventy-six after quick, prodigious beginnings. Wordsworth was eighty when he died, Ruskin eighty-one – both early starters. Proust patrolled his world but scarcely left his room in maturity to do so, and may be that is why he managed his work in a lifetime of only fifty-one years. We honour the great creative individuals who die young, but there is a greatness that goes with plenitude: Michelangelo's eighty-nine years and J. S. Bach's seventy-five, rarities then, Goethe's eighty-three, in our own time and country Ben Nicholson and Henry Moore, both at work until they were eighty-eight.

Between Turner and the twentieth century there is much British art of interest and much to be said about it all, yet little to glory in. Passions and convictions yes but, with rare exceptions, achievements in which these are muted or confused. Palmer's long career (he lived 1805–81) climaxed early after a prodigious beginning. We associate him with Shoreham in Kent but he was there for only six years and a central Londoner for the rest. Blake, very much a Londoner too, was his inspiration and model but he knew him only a very short time. That was enough for Palmer's visionary momentum: Blake's burning energy countered the constraints of upbringing and training and turned directionless eccentricity into a spell in Paradise. A brief spell, certainly. Before he was thirty Palmer felt himself, as his biographer puts it,

'expelled from Paradise . . . outside the wall of the locked sacred garden'. There had been conviction and joy: 'God worked in great love with my spirit last night', he wrote to himself in 1826. There followed a loss of faith in most things: 'the sad realities of life blot the field of vision', he wrote in a letter of 1835.

Attempts to build new art on his best examples in mid-century England perhaps had to fail, not least because of this element of escapism. The Pre-Raphaelites said they were reaching back to the quattrocento, as Palmer had reached back to German and Flemish primitives, but they neither did it enough nor to the aspects that could then have served painting best. It was the semi-foreigner among them, Rossetti, whose art looks strongest today, perhaps because he had educated Italian parents, more surely because he, brother to Christina and a convinced poet himself, did not need to overload his art with verbal baggage. Whistler, the American European with keen Oriental interests and a deft spinner of words when he wanted them, knew better than anyone what art was best at and where flights of the literary imagination should be kept out, and Ruskin hated him for it. Partly thanks to this unEnglish certainty, his work is unchallengeable in its time and place. Not plenitude in his case but marksmanship. He died at sixty-nine. Holman Hunt's much longer career – he died aged eighty-three – is full of dutiful and sometimes innovatory practices and fine ideals, but his work lost much of its interest (which is not to say ambition or energy) after the 1850s, when it still had a half-century to run.

Foreign impulses came slowly and were soon disarmed. Did Impressionism ever really take root here? The vividness of Constable and Turner had spoiled it for us, and perhaps Ruskin's prophetic words, which seem to have spurred on the French, made the English feel they knew it all already. And Post-Impressionism? Was it not a great misfortune that it should have been Roger Fry and his friends who, rather late in the day, rubbed English noses in the art of Cézanne, Gauguin, Van Gogh, Matisse and early Picasso? Cézanne became the preferred hero, especially for Fry, but there is little in Bloomsbury art to say they were apt disciples. Isolated paintings and drawings show Vanessa Bell or Duncan Grant reaching out for primitivist aspects of Gauguin or Matisse, but most of the time they were content with an art of easy looking. Sickert and the painters gathered round him in successive groups remained attached to modified forms of Impressionism, though some of them, Gilman especially, found ways of packing pictures more tightly with form and colour as a way of moving on from Impressionism's sketchiness to a more positive, more modern surface.

By 1900 urban life was normal life. Peasants had now become agricultural labourers, manpower of an industry that rapidly industrialised. Ploughshares were beaten into tractors, scythes into combine harvesters. The face of the countryside changed rapidly, to mechanised agriculture and also to urban and suburban encroachments – the suburbs themselves being right-hearted, wrong-headed attempts to allow the urban worker some glimpse of the natural world. For the more prosperous urbanite the countryside serves as a complementary lifestyle; for the less advantaged, as an occasional escape. If there are still rural societies they are now likely to be 'mining communities', neither countryfolk nor townfolk quite, clustered around and serving what to the rest of us look like satanic mills. Dennis Skinner, in a parliamentary debate on the threatened closure of coal-mines, spoke of the bond that exists between the miner and the earth in which he tunnels. It seems that this form of rural existence too is to go, making room for the new power stations, gleaming, imposed rather than grown sources of miraculously engendered energy in which robot routines and long-spoon handling is overseen by small teams of humans armed to the teeth against work which threatens not only them but the entire environment in which they exist as aliens, not only locally but whole regions, countries, continents.

Such thoughts propose new views of the countryside, too vast and too radical to be accommodated in the old town/country duality. National bodies buy up whole stretches of 'unspoilt' land as reserves: bits of near-nature denaturised by their isolation from the rest. Others watch over our common right to walk on other portions of the land, if not to put our horses, cows or geese on it, and it takes something like a permanent crusade to guard those rights. The cities retain the glamour of artificiality even as they become more monotonously alike: they continue as prime centres of cultural production and consumption, seats of power and of some sorts of pleasure. 'Flâneurs' of

the Baudelaire and Walter Benjamin type survive, sipping the flavours of city life as butterflies taste the nectar of meadows and gardens. One feels their days are numbered. We all know that cities are places also of isolation, of self-exile and of exclusion.

The most compelling urban story I know is that of the empty city. There are several versions of it, in books and films, and it has been with me from childhood. You awake to find your city deserted, everyone gone except you, driven or sucked out by some unknown disaster or threat of disaster. Everything still works. All the treats and satisfactions of what is now an open city, untrammelled by prohibitions, are now available to you free – until you and time have exhausted them, or until whatever force removed all the people around you comes for you too. Meanwhile you are an urban Robinson Crusoe. For the moment the city is the new paradise, more fairground than Garden of Eden, until the machine stops.

There is no satisfactory ending to that story, as there is none to Crusoe's. For us, fingers crossed, the city system more or less works, neither quite the blind oppression itself Kafka pictured, nor the Unanimist world of benign mass interaction that Jules Romains and others celebrated at the start of our century. The city is on the one hand the mortal sin that Richard Jefferies, a farmer's son, saw it as – his novel *After London* (1885) has 'all that mighty heart' Wordsworth exulted over turned into a poisonous swamp – and, on the other, the site of progress towards Utopia that revolutionaries and artists have often claimed it to be. Capitalism both rears and kills the city, making of it a tool to be dropped every evening. Computerised communication and roboticised production advance. Will some future Oliver Goldsmith hymn The Deserted City? What shall we have lost?

Our view of the city is ambiguous now while our view of the country (though the word is deeply ambiguous) is dangerously simple. I doubt that there are people in England who can be considered rustic today, in the sense that their understanding of it is governed by rural experience alone. If an exception is possible, he or she would have to be a primitive: someone like Alfred Wallis, the ex-fisherman, ex-chandler, born close to the sea at Devonport, who lived in Penzance and St Ives and was discovered painting there in 1928, at the age of seventy-three, by two youngish professionals, Ben

Nicholson and Christopher Wood. Wallis's world was whole and seamless: land, sea, houses and streets, quays and lighthouses, boats and ships old and new, visualised with childlike directness and with unclouded clarity of recollection. He painted out of his head without doubt or hesitation, and the only primitive thing about his work was that he did not choose his style. He painted 'for company', his wife having died, and recked nothing of art. His attention was untrammelled and simple.

All the rest of us are now double men. Wilfred Mellers calls Vaughan Williams 'the double man' because of the way he grasped town and country firmly: the *Sea Symphony* was followed by the Unanimist *London Symphony* and the lyrical *Pastoral Symphony*, earthy and spiritual in turn. There are many other dualities in Vaughan Williams that could interest us – his Christian agnosticism, his attachment to Rossetti and to Whitman, his use of Bunyan and Nietzsche, his professional debts to Delius and to Tudor polyphony. We can all be pulled in what seem opposite directions. In Vaughan Williams these pairs thrive as energies to which his creative powers respond. He was born a country boy but grew up a Londoner and, while he was profoundly an Englishman and owed exceptionally little to foreign, which then meant German, musical models, he was no little Englander. If there was an inclination to national self-sufficiency in the choices that shaped his idiom, behind them was a wide and historically deep world of modes and rhythms.

But we could argue that neither of his worlds, the urban or the rustic, was real and now, nor meant to be. Vaughan Williams was a visionary, another figure in that English tradition I have mentioned and to which he would have had me add Thomas Traherne. Romanticism ends in making us see everything in mythical terms, town as well as country, new as well as old. The all-embracing myth is that of the apocalypse, the final transformation and transubstantiation of everything. Thoughts of the apocalypse pervaded modern Europe before the First World War and are arising now once more, on what should be a global scale, as we have had to begin to face the sudden or gradual destruction of our habitat, through willed destruction or abuse, as well as the apparent failure of the political systems we tried to pin our faith on, capitalism or communism or democratic constitutions.

The apocalypse revealed in the Bible leads on to a Third Testament of rest in paradise or to eternal damnation. The apocalypse of the beginning of our century ambiguously proposed the rapid evolution of human consciousness after a century of materialism or, associated with it rather than as alternative, the successful revolution of the masses against autocracy and oligarchy. In either case, liberation was on offer and gave a tone of exaltation to the many forms in which the apocalypse was announced. Today exaltation is difficult to sustain and rarely met.

The country as spiritual home and healing image remains our resource, and the question is now not of insider and outsider, Constable or Turner, but rather of affinities and distances. These can sometimes be explained in terms of birth and normal residence, but the town/country duality hardly exists in England now. We choose our mental territories. Delius, the Bradford boy, in his youth consumed whole tracts of the world, from Germany, Scandinavia and France to Florida and Manhattan, and attached himself to broad swathes of creative expression, Whitman, Nietzsche, Munch, Post-Impressionism (Gauguin's *Nevermore* hung over his desk), Rodin, Strindberg and the poems and stories of Jens Peter Jacobsen (which Nielsen and Schoenberg also used). From 1897 on, when he was thirty-seven, until his death in 1934, Delius lived at Grez-sur-Loing, near Fontainebleau, in Barbizon School and Impressionism land. His typical music was rhapsodic and rural, and most of it was composed in his house and garden at Grez. His basic training was German; that established, he fed Negro and English folksong elements into forms of Wagnerian fluidity, using the chromaticism of Wagner and Grieg and producing orchestral sounds of remarkable subtlety that owe something to Debussy. He was rural by inclination, but also cosmopolitan and a citizen of the world. His music takes us into realms far from urban realities.

David Bomberg, born in Birmingham of Polish immigrant parents and raised in Cardiff and from the age of five in London's East End, was certainly a Londoner and an urbanite more than anything else. He was trained at the Slade and drawn to Sickert, and then he was suddenly infected by Cubism and Futurism. Associated with Vorticism, he became one of the world's most adventurous and intelligent modernists and would have been honoured as such in any other country but this. The war broke both his career and Vorticism. Subsequently, British lack of interest in his later work came close to breaking him. For many reasons Bomberg in the 1920s became a kind of Expressionist, but one for whom realising the physical presence of his model or motif was the goal, and with it, secondarily but necessarily, recording his particular awareness of or sensibility to the subject – not a solipsistic use of the external world as a mirror for himself. The result was images of the external world, landscapes often but also still-lifes and portraits, in which paint as a structural medium has equal weight with the seen object. The art student who had gained prizes for drawing found new ways of drawing with the loaded brush and with his gesture and bodily weight as part of the medium. Sight knowledge is turned into paint knowledge. David Sylvester said in 1964 of Bomberg's painting that it was 'not a painting of structure, but the painting of the discovering of structure'. Gill Polonsky, writing about Bomberg in 1990, emphasised his need, and his recognition of that need, to 'perpetuate in some form of imagery his inward spiritual urge to a higher and more complete existence', as he wrote in 1937. She claims that this belief in art as the means of achieving transcendental purposes set him apart from artists around him and deprived him of success in his time.

The important point for us here is that he achieved his goal primarily through landscape, moreover landscapes seen, drawn and painted almost always abroad, in Palestine and Spain mostly. The young avant-gardist who had produced powerful semi-abstract and abstract work that combined significant subject-matter with 'a new constructive geometrical art' (as the influential philosopher-critic T. E. Hulme called it in 1914, pointing to this as the only way for art to progress), now appeared to have rejected subject-matter in favour of selected natural motifs. For the last three years of his life, until he died in 1957, he lived and worked at Ronda in the mountains of Andalusia, where he had painted earlier, in 1934–35. His powerful Cubist/Futurist paintings of 1912–14 were abstractions of named and significant figure subjects, finally distilled beyond legibility. But in spite of superficial similarities in his work to the Vorticist art of Wyndham Lewis, William Roberts, Wadsworth and

others, Bomberg was an isolated figure. Among modernists at large, only Kandinsky, Malevich and Picabia insisted comparably on both abstraction and content at this time. In England only Epstein, who fashioned his alarming *Rock Drill* in 1913, showed equal conviction. One is tempted to say that in his more naturalistic landscapes Bomberg inverted this emphasis: now, not content (meaning the deeper communication of the image, not just its named subject) but form, expression of an abstract sort through energetic, legible forms that reflect and convincingly deliver an observed scene. But of course the form and its delivery as experienced is the content of the work, and what makes Bomberg a true son of Cézanne has nothing to do with Cubism but with this finding of the exact point where the motif, the painter's living with the motif and a fully functioning pictorial construction meet in tripartite balance.

Though the results are so different, much the same could be said of Ben Nicholson's landscapes. Thinking of his white reliefs of the 1930s, which many have called Constructivist (whether or not that went with approval), one does not hesitate to call him an urbanite. Bomberg did his early work in London: 'I look upon *Nature*, while I live in a *steel city*', he wrote in 1914 in the catalogue of his first one-man show; '. . . my object is the *construction of Pure Form*'. In 1934 and 1937, when Nicholson was beginning and then becoming known for those reliefs, geometrical forms painted white, he must have irritated his friends and puzzled those who thought the reliefs mindless ornaments by offering little by way of explanation of his dramatic development away from still-lifes and landscapes other than '"painting" and "religious experience" are the same thing'. All around him artists were saying sensible things, such as that what they called Constructive art painting and design demonstrated an international language soon to be the shared visual language of a harmoniously developed modern world. Nicholson claimed a higher role than that for his art, and in this he was close to Bomberg.

They knew and respected each other and were certainly friends in the early 1920s when Nicholson was making his late start in painting. In 1911–12 he had been at the Slade, Bomberg's contemporary. Then there was an interval in which one imagines the not so young Benjamin (sixteen to seventeen when at the Slade but twenty-four in 1920) wrestling with the question whether he could possibly be a painter when both his parents were. In 1920 he married a painter, Winifred, and became one. And in the 1930s, then partnering Barbara Hepworth, he became one of the few leading avant-garde figures in British art and the most compelling among them. He not only associated with Naum Gabo, the Russian modernist who had come to London from Moscow via years in Berlin and Paris, but was seen as representing the broader Russian/Soviet move into three-dimensional geometrical abstract art. His white reliefs were exhibited in Britain's first and for a long time only international exhibition of abstract art – Nicolete Gray's Abstract and Concrete exhibition, shown in Oxford, Cambridge, Liverpool and London in 1936 – alongside Mondrian. Altogether he looked like the sharp edge of an avant-garde wholly devoted to urban and cosmopolitan ideals and intent on destroying English traditionalism.

Yet Nicholson's home, by birth and preference, was the countryside and he spent most of his life in it while keeping an eye on London and Paris. Born in the village of Denham, he lived in many places in childhood and youth as the Nicholsons moved around southern England, settling for periods in Chaucer's House, just outside Blenheim Palace, then at 1 Pilgrim's Lane in Hampstead, close to the Heath, and on to Mecklenburgh Square in Bloomsbury and then the vicarage in Rottingdean, while father William disappeared to his studio in London to woo society and paint its portraits. Ben's professional life spanned sixty-two years and forty-four of those were spent in rural settings of exceptional interest. He chose to live in Cumberland and the Ticino with Winifred Nicholson, in London and Cornwall with Barbara Hepworth and in the Ticino with his third wife, Felicitas Vogler. In his late seventies he returned to England, to Great Shelford outside Cambridge, exulting in the peace and beauty of the place. His very last years, aged eighty and more, he spent at 2a Pilgrim's Lane, diagonally across from where he had lived as a child. He was always an avid traveller. For health and study reasons he travelled widely in his youth, and there were visits to Italy and France in the 1920s and 1930s. From the 1950s on he could afford to go anywhere, but it was almost always to country places, in Turkey for example, or the

Greek Islands, or the smaller towns of Italy (Urbino, Siena) and the land between them, and to Cumberland and Yorkshire from the Ticino.

His art took the form of still-life and landscape. The white reliefs can be called abstracted still-lifes; his later reliefs, from the late 1950s on, were abstracted landscapes. I must add that this summary would not have pleased him, though he admitted occasionally to the still-life basis of the white reliefs and in his titles often drew attention to the landscape experiences related to his later and often much larger reliefs. Yet they were certainly not scenic views processed by abstraction. They were assemblages of board and paint into which he condensed experiences of being in and moving through landscape: time is an important element in them including the seasonal movements of nature. But he would not have wanted anyone to draw a hard line between abstract art and figurative, especially not in his own case, and he found a neat way of erasing any possible demarcation between still-life and landscape. In a four-sentence statement he wrote in 1957 for an ICA show he welcomed Action painting, said that non-figurative painting always had a source in nature and that idea and form are inseparable, and ended with: 'My "still life" paintings are closely identified with landscape, more closely than are my landscapes which related perhaps more to "still life".'

Many of his paintings combine a still-life group of typical Nicholson objects – mugs, goblets, jugs – and a landscape, often the hills, occasional houses and sea around the St Ives he knew so well. The still-life/landscape combination has a long history. Winifred Nicholson used it frequently. The duality, tangible and near backed by intangible and far, domestic and outside world, small and large, could be underlined by stylistic contrast or counteracted by giving much the same account of both parts and by mingling their forms.

Yet Nicholson also transformed landscape to bring it to table, so to speak. In his early work a farmhouse, a paddock, trees, fences, hills and sky could be brought close and set out without any apparent violation of nature's light and space as a quietly lyrical arrangement. In both his still-lifes and his landscapes, already then, he used to the full mature Cubism's invitation to construct an image on a surface, and also to confound the eye with spatial complexities that counter any perspectival expectations we might still have. The white reliefs too are spatial conundrums – not at all the move from 'illusionistic' to 'real' space they are often mistaken for. In the 1950s a great series of often large paintings explores still-life arrangements as the ground bass for elaborate linear polyphonies. And then come the late reliefs, including some of his largest and most powerful works and embodying a wide range of formal developments and colour and texture treatments. Looking over the lake to the mountains opposite his Ticino house, driving through the Alps and the Apennines and flying over mountains, seas and islands, watching the snow settle, drift and melt and the rocks resume their reign, filled him with much the same wonder as the effortless, accurate swoop of a particular bird into a particular part of a bush, a cat's ritual pirouette on always the same spot in a room, the instinctively right trajectory a great tennis player would choose for his ball.

These are lay concerns unless we can allow some superior, even supernatural, meaning to this kind of unconscious rightness. Nicholson's personal image was that of a cool, intelligent, neat and athletic man, with the Englishman's (in spite of Scots and French blood in him) preference for a quip rather than a personal confession. Yet the visionary urge in him is clear, unmitigated in his white reliefs, accompanied by earthly delights in his other work. Perhaps it is most easily seen and felt in his best drawings and prints when a line soars like song or a bird to reach the exact spot where, meeting another, it creates space on the paper and at the same time speaks of Nicholson's intimate passion for the cloisters at Torcello, the corners of two houses on Patmos, the curves of a jug and a bottle and for what his line can do with them. He worked ceaselessly, everything had to yield to work, but that work included long periods of looking and of assimilation without conscious study. Before drawing a place he would live with it for hours. Before knowing his own work he would need to live with it for days or weeks. He said a work of art is a force that transforms the world, and reckoned he knew whether what he had done was good only when it had hung a while in the corner, being assimilated unconsciously as part of the room's quality of life. The finished work radiates energies but is also the focus of energies – not all of them, he would have said, the artist's own.

Thinking of Nicholson's line helps one close the gap one assumes between his art and Bomberg's. Both attended closely to their motifs in order to transcend them; both made the fullest use of their chosen media; both, however rich the result, aimed at an economical, concentrated statement. Used to pictures as paint on canvas, we readily accept Bomberg's use of paint as part of a tradition that goes back to Titian; too readily, probably. In an age in which art has included all sorts of materials and processes, from detritus to nothing, we accept too readily Nicholson's building up of cut boards and often quite limited colours and textures to confront us with mighty images that confound the eye for all their physicality. The progressives' preference, in the 1920s and 1930s, was for an Arcadian lyricism typified by much Bloomsbury painting, on which admiration for Post-Impressionism and Fauvism left little mark and which generally pretended that Cubism had never happened, let alone city life. The innocence of intellectuals leaves a lot to be desired. It ended in charm and, in reaction perhaps to Pre-Raphaelitism's high moralities, left art frankly decorative. Everything Bomberg and Nicholson did distances them from that false simplicity.

Paul Nash too. Nash and Nicholson were close friends from 1911 on, and especially in the 1920s and 1930s. Nash was one of the few able to see the white reliefs for what they were, a profound innovation in art, 'the discovery of something like a new world', as he wrote in 1935. They had worked together at Dymchurch in 1923 (where the Nashes then lived) and in Cumberland in 1925 (the Nicholsons' home). In 1933–34 Ben Nicholson and Barbara Hepworth were in Nash's Unit One group and exhibition, together with a surprisingly large range of other painters (Armstrong, Burra, Hillier etc), one other sculptor, Henry Moore, and the architects Wells Coates and Colin Lucas. Nicholson was obviously troubled by the catholicity of Nash's list, especially in the light of Nash's stated intention to effect a marriage of the most advanced English art with new developments in architectural and other design. He was probably troubled also by Nash's ventures out of an English-based sometimes visionary mode, Rossetti plus Blake, into de Chirico's metaphysical dreamworld and then his open embrace of Surrealism. Nash could not of course participate in the Abstract and Concrete exhibition or in

Circle: international survey of constructive art, published in 1937 and edited by Nicholson, Gabo and the architect J. L. Martin as a counter to Surrealism's bid to take over the English avant-garde. Nicholson always kept his warm feelings for Nash but had little to say about his art.

In some ways they were opposites. Both men had health problems and personal and domestic difficulties; art was their strong defence as well as their way of identifying themselves to themselves. Both responded to the magic light and nature and to human marvels such as the standing stones of Avebury (Nash) or Penwith and Carnac (Nicholson). What they did with them was significantly different. Nash set the megaliths and nature against each other as past and present, with the stones as vestiges of a human race long gone; the image is pessimistic, negatively apocalyptic. Nicholson's stones are now. They march across the landscape of Cornwall and Brittany and he imagined them going on to Russia and beyond. He neither drew them nor painted them, but built them into his 1960s reliefs. Nash teaches one what is always absent from Nicholson's range of work, arguably even from the last works in which some see an element of foreboding, and that is death and death's double, nostalgia. Nash's landscapes become more visionary over the years and are thus able to speak eloquently of dramatic encounters, including war. In the end his sunflowers and the sun itself portend a twilight of the gods.

Nash's art was first illustrative and literary, and turned towards landscape via his intimacy with the garden at Iver Heath in Buckinghamshire, where the Nash family had moved when he was two. He lived at various country addresses after years at school and at the Slade in London: at Dymchurch in Kent during 1920–25, at Rye in Sussex 1931–33, near Swanage in Dorset 1934–36. But he knew himself to be a Londoner, fascinated by London's 'thousand facets and incalculable moods'. If not the only he is the best example of a modern English artist confronting nature as a Romantic, steeped in Blake, in Sir Thomas Browne's treatise on the funeral arrangements of the ancients, *Urn Burial* (1685), and in the heavily symbolist plays of his friend Gordon Bottomley. He could design a dazzlingly modern bathroom for Edward James's flighty dancer wife, Tilly Losch, all mirrors and chrome and better-than-Bauhaus geometry, so hi-tec and

go ahead that one mistakes it for a brilliant film set rather than a real place. For the rest he used landscape as a poetic vehicle for the tensions that abused his body all his life. It is interesting that in writing about Blake in 1932 he emphasised that Blake was 'said to have hated nature, and his work certainly shows a contempt for natural appearances. Like the surrealists of today he sought material for his pictures in other worlds. . . . The finest [of his images] burn with unreal life and seem the product of unique vision.' Revealing too is Nash's cross reaction to his pupil Richard Seddon's water-colour of a skating pond, around 1914. At first silent, obviously irritated, he then burst out with: 'You've wrecked it! The best pictures do not have people in them!'

Nash's first works had people in them, bloodless creatures in the Pre-Raphaelite vein. Then landscape could stand for bodies, Whittenham Clumps for example, round and full. But that passed too and there is nothing sensuous about the landscapes that followed. His gardens are haunted; his seas are dead even when they are not made of broken warplanes, his landscapes speak of the coming apocalypse when they do not suggest it has already done its work, leaving nature to wind up her work. Like Blake and other Romantics, he looks forward by looking back. His art is not about the past but rather about what will be; its mode refers us to a dreamed, lost glory.

Ivon Hitchens painted the present glory of the world – of a limited world he knew intimately and in which he was literally at home. He was a Londoner until he and his wife were bombed out of their flat in 1940 and decided to disappear into a particularly serene part of Sussex, Lavington Common, a little to the south of Petworth where Turner had been Lord Egremont's guest in the 1820s and 1830s. There is something Thoreau-like about this move, but it was for keeps. Ivon and Mary Hitchens lived in a caravan, then built a house in a tract of woodland and created a large pond. For years, with little interruption, he painted what he saw around him there in a spirit of innocent marvelling. He and Nicholson had been good friends, in the mid-1920s and early 1930s. Hitchens brought Nicholson into the Seven and Five Society which Nicholson subsequently pressed into abstraction, destroying it in the process. This ended their closeness. In 1925 Hitchens had come up to Cumberland to stay with Ben and Winifred Nicholson. He had there produced fresh, luminous paintings of interiors and flowers, including one very much of a Ben-and-Winifred sort, a pot of flowers on the window and a broad view of the landscape beyond.

The spontaneity and lightness with which he painted then surfaced again in his Sussex landscapes. The most immediate characteristic of the mature Hitchens painting is its format – more than twice as wide as it is high. We can associate this with the tradition of marine painting, or with Turner's paintings at Petworth, or with both. In any case, it is not one standard size or ratio but varies with different occasions and it led him to develop a pictorial structure that belongs neither to seascapes nor to Turner. Sussex, this format and his amazingly fluent style came together in images that hover between description and abstraction, and also between naturalistic recording and recreated visions. The broad stage of his canvas lent itself to subdivision, and in many paintings we sense two-section, at times three-section arrangements. These enable him to accommodate multiple interests and pleasures without bringing them into conflict. One half of the image might be close and closed, while the other is deep and open. The space sometimes seems to curve, as indeed it might for the painter scanning a panorama. In his three-part compositions, the central area is likely not to be dominant (as it would be in a traditional triptych) but to offer a transition between two views. In fact the fluency, the pleasure and energy we sense in Hitchens's use of paint, in sonorous and sometimes in bright colours, broadly applied and transforming nature's forms into vivid pictorial events, screens stage management of a very sophisticated and inventive sort. Hitchens choreographed nature on to his canvases. Between the scene and the presentation lie several steps of transformation. The freshness of the final image persuades us that it was easy, the work of a happy moment, and that moment is just now: beware, wet paint.

The same question, of what one might call the time-direction of their art, helps one to focus on Nicholson and Stanley Spencer. Nicholson cared not at all for Spencer's work and claimed never to have met him though they were contemporaries at the Slade. (Spencer commuted daily from Cookham. Nicholson claimed to have spent his Slade time playing billiards at a nearby hotel. He exaggerated, but it is quite possible he never encountered Spencer, three years ahead of himself and presumably in another group.) That Spencer in his remarkable way combined keen naturalism with a wholly visionary approach is now well known, also that he could at times be a harsh, perplexed realist of the Neue Sachlichkeit sort, most painfully so in his paintings of Patricia Preece and himself.

A severe naturalism, almost an emphatic, critical realism, is basic to his landscape paintings too. His prime task was to stage the Bible in Cookham and to locate the dramas and longings of his own life within the Bible's fertile narratives or as home-made extensions of them. That involved methods derived from pre-Renaissance Italian frescoes and from Indian temple sculpture, as well as a caricatural reinventing of the human image that comes out of Pre-Raphaelite drawing. Like the Pre-Raphaelite Brotherhood he was a designer more than a painter, fascinated by the detail of grass and dresses, of hawsers, sheet steel and rivets, of fences and pubic hair, and he painted them more to show us exactly how those things are than to show us what he can do with paint. That said, he can surprise us with occasional impastos and flourishes. In his paintings of fields and meadows around Cookham and of Cookham gardens, he demonstrates an attachment to here and now and to a hard focus that gives them hypnotic qualities usually associated with trompe l'oeil paintings. His narrative paintings (fusing the history and genre categories) speak of the future even when their stories lie in the past, his landscapes of an eternal present. Surprisingly, they are devoid of people. 'A place is incomplete without a person', he said. Yet his landscape paintings are crowded with signs of human occupation. Standing before them we become Spencer the observer and Spencer the occupant, drawn in by the obsessional detail. It seems only apt that he should have been born in a straggly village close to more villages and to small and large towns and not far from metropolitan London, and that all his life Cookham remained the essential centre of his life and his vision. The Pre-Raphaelites had to labour in Palestine to picture the Bible. Like a medieval or a Renaissance painter, Spencer knew that the real world of his day was the only proper setting for it. And so the natural and ordinary setting he knew so intimately takes on a special radiance as the place where the human and divine will meet tomorrow.

While English painting mostly hesitated between Edwardian glamour and varieties of disarmed modernisms, sculpture took on the role of pathfinder. Not sculpture in general, of course; dependent on site and commissions more than painting, it did not then seem possible to most sculptors to do more than serve naturalism efficiently and undemandingly and let questions of style look after themselves. Gaudier-Brzeska and Epstein, a Frenchman and an American from Paris, brought in attitudes and techniques that frightened the English public then and could well still do so now. Primitivism of form plus direct carving summarises much of what they did, and in Epstein's case we should add an insistence on significant subject-matter: sex, birth, life, death, imaged without apology or decoration. They and Roger Fry's mind- and eye-opening essays on primitive forms of art, together with his subsequent experience of such things in the British Museum and in Paris, made it possible for the young Henry Moore to associate his professional ambitions with the need to reground sculpture in basic human experience and in basic sculptural processes. What he was taught was almost exclusively modelling and the idealised naturalism of the academies; what he did from the start, whilst still a student, was to carve in a way that explored the material (almost exclusively stone at this time) and to carve subjects that to him were basic: female figures and occasionally human masks and animals.

By the end of the 1920s, when he was about thirty and his colleagues at the Royal College of Art were demanding his dismissal for bringing art into disrepute, he had homed in on the subjects that would remain central to him: Mother and Child and the Reclining Figure. He had made powerful Mother and Child sculptures already in 1924 and 1925 and had then begun to explore the Reclining Figure, achieving what still seems his first fully fledged sculpture, at once personal and a compendium of whole swathes of sculptural history, European and exotic, his *Reclining Figure* of 1929 in Leeds.

Landscape surfaces in Moore's thinking in two ways: in his wish to see his larger works set into landscape and in his exploration of the female figure, the Reclining Figure especially, as a simulacrum of nature. He relates them both to his native Yorkshire. He was born in Castleford, an industrial town, but Yorkshire's rich, often dramatic landscape was close and part of his childhood experience. His father was a miner, and the sculptor may have assimilated from him something of the miner's intimacy with the earth. His mother was a strong woman, in character and physique, the benign despot of eight children of whom she asked Henry, the seventh, to rub her back with liniment to ease her rheumatism. Along with the rocks thrusting out of the earth at Adel all this would seem enough by way of basis for a career in sculpture, especially if we add as a key impulse young Henry's awareness of Michelangelo, the greatest sculptor in the long history of art and also the man who achieved unparalleled greatness through sculpture.

Most people, women as well as men, recognise the Reclining Figure/landscape analogy. It may lie at the core of our ancient notion that landscape is our mother, feeding and comforting us, but also a challenge as we grow, almost a sexual encounter. Such feelings lie nearer some surfaces than others. Constable had little interest in powerful, sublime nature; Turner cared more for fishing than for agriculture, his pictures tell us, and would rather have the fishermen foundering than hauling in an easy catch. Palmer and Nash are closer to Moore's position than Nicholson and Spencer. Constable and Nicholson celebrate the light and life of nature as an emanation of divinity and are filled with joy by transient effects of sunshine and moistness; Turner, Nash and Moore are more gravely focused on symbolism and there is a pessimistic force in their expression. From early on Moore emphasised the importance of 'Observation of Natural Objects', partly because it was indeed an aspect of his work and perhaps to reassure a public distanced by anything non-representational that nature remained his guide.

I walked long ago in one of the Yorkshire Dales and was seized by the sense of its being a female body. Moore's Reclining Figures incorporate landscape forms, here and there or all-over, and the references shift as the forms and materials of his art changed. In 1924, writing to William Rothenstein, principal of the Royal College of Art, Moore said that it seemed to him that 'it is modelling that has sapped the manhood out of Western sculpture'. After 1945 modelling dominated his work and by giving him sole control of form tended to weaken it. None the less, among his best works of any time are the two- and three-part bronze Reclining Figures done in 1959 and after. Adel Rocks appear in the first of them and then cliff forms dominate (and one wonders whether they came direct from nature, from Dorset, the Isle of Wight or wherever, or via Courbet and Monet). They bring grandeur and rugged strength to these sculptures. The Mother and Child theme recurred at intervals, most obviously when Henry and Irena Moore at last became parents with the birth of Mary in 1946, just when he had been working on the *Madonna and Child* for Northampton and drawing and modelling Family Groups. It is not a theme wholly separate from the Reclining Figures. The more grandiose of these give me, at any rate, the feeling of being the child in the work as much as the wanderer in the landscape.

The truth-to-materials doctrine, from which Epstein, Moore and then others started, combined with abstraction to give sculpture new functions in art, from constructed steel or moulded plastics without bases to performance art, land art and the sculptor's use or abuse of his own body. The results were not always what the opening had promised; that is how art moves on. Caro's rugged, agricultural-looking constructions were followed by much lighter and more elegant works in bright colours or metals. At times they referred directly to landscape; at others they evoked it merely. *Prairie* (1967) would be compelling in any colour. Painted in two tones of matt yellow and given that name it easily speaks of great plains with little to interrupt their horizontality. Nothing moves; there is duration and there is a sense of spread, the four long horizontal tubes taking us to where the sky meets the land. In other colours it would presumably bring other associations. Very much as in music we need in abstract art some clues to how we should engage our imaginations.

This is where land art operates directly and specifically. Much has been written, and well written, about the work of artists who have worked in and with landscape as site and material, as opposed to picturing or otherwise recreating it by traditional means of art. What needs stressing is that another class of objects results, calling for different approaches. The Boyle Family's transcriptions of randomly selected patches of the face of the earth in this respect are close to traditional art. The magic and might of the relief replicas they make stem from their mysterious exactness and the history painting scale, and from their permanence, whereas nature itself is always in transition as well as seen under transient conditions. In theory we might find the same majesty in the source material. In practice we would walk over the same ground, pass by the same cliff, without necessarily giving them a second glance. It is the separating out that accords aesthetic value; the more unremarkable the motif the greater the gain. The same might be said to apply to painted landscape, but there we know beforehand we are to suspend disbelief and accept a visual paraphrase in paint on canvas, not an exact replication. Ruskin supervised John Brett when the younger man painted the *Val d'Aosta* with photographic precision. It was shown at the Royal Academy in 1859 and Ruskin praised it as the first landscape painting to give us 'the power of visiting a place, reasoning about it, and knowing it', and then, perhaps to his own surprise, added that, for all the exact description it offers and which Ruskin re-enacts in words, it is not 'a noble picture': 'I never saw the mirror so held up to Nature; but it is Mirror's work, not Man's.' Yet it is also 'a wonder of toil and delicate handling'. That is true too of the typical Boyle relief, and I cannot quite understand why it should not strike me as mere 'Mirror's work'. Is it that Brett's account, being a paraphrase and thus not impersonal, calls for a voice, whereas the Boyle transcription gains from its silence? Yet the Boyles's work, especially seen in quantity, feels far from impersonal. There is something headlong about its appropriation of the world whilst leaving it undisturbed. That, one realises, is one of the powers of art: it takes without taking away.

Often it adds, as Cézanne's added to Provence. Richard Long's rearrangements of landscape, minimal in themselves, maximal in the mark left on the site, more or less temporarily, are another kind of appropriation. I think of his actions as gentle and self-effacing, and yet they do say 'I was here', or 'someone was here' at the very least, and this someone was sentient and consciously creative. Long brings geometry as his gift to nature (the Boyles's rectangles are expedients, aesthetically negative).

When he brings stones and other parts of nature into a gallery his geometry functions quite differently, confronting the gallery's own shape and scale and restraining the stones, sticks or mud. A neat circle of disjointed fragments of stone is a powerful statement indoors largely because the stones and the circle are at odds. A path cleared of stone in Bolivia is a line first and an absence of stones second, a softer statement, less disruption, and the more poetic in consequence.

Richard Long was born and lives in Bristol. No longer England's second largest city, Bristol gives ready access to the countryside and Long began his sculpting of nature in the mid 1960s when he was still a student. David Nash, his coeval, was born in suburban Esher, studied in Brighton, Kingston and Chelsea, and in his early twenties removed himself to Blaenau Ffestiniog in North Wales where he has been more or less continuously ever since. He had put down roots of affection through family visits from childhood on. The mountain immediately behind his home and workplace, a former chapel, is covered in discarded slate, a monument to one sort of man/nature interaction. Raw nature surrounds the place, and he legally owns a small patch of it. Humanly he owns it all, as we too do except that only intimacy and respect give access to it.

Long and Nash admire each other's work and my words must not force them into opposition, but there are contrasts worth noting. There is something of the commando about Long's incursions into Peru, Dartmoor, Iceland, Bolivia, Scotland, Nepal, Africa, wherever, whether to make a mark and take photographs, or patrol an invested path, or record in brief notes or single words the encounters of a given time. On these occasions he takes nothing away materially; one senses he takes much away mentally from these intense engagements. When he removes stones, twigs, logs, mud this is a marginal borrowing, no robbery. They act for him in the galleries of the world, but that feels a temporary engagement even when they are bought. It is easy to imagine them coming home from the cities one day, redistributed from the bowels of the Hayward Gallery and other such strongholds where they are stored with care, suspended for a while from the routines of erosion and decay that is their natural fate. Perhaps, like Picasso's bicycle-seat-plus-handlebars *Bull's Head*, they should one day be recycled.

Installed in the galleries they remain visitors, Long's troupe of repertory actors, performing brilliantly the tableaux vivants he choreographs for them.

David Nash's work with living, growing plants and with fresh timber cut down not for him but from practical necessity, speaks in a different voice and of different things. He plants, tends and shapes trees. He cuts up trees, making a broad range of sculptural objects from them, and sculptural events like the ovens in which he turns left-over twigs into charcoal to draw with. No waste, but not total transformation. The movement of his sculptures over time as atmosphere works on the wood in the galleries is part of the life of that wood though a different process from the one it would undergo in the forest. Cutting the tree into many things sounds like removing all tree-ness, but in experience this is not so. The edge of a bowl is and restates the circumference of the trunk. His branch constructions bring man's making and nature's into confrontation, the branches keeping their natural, unkempt character while coming together to form tables, chairs, cubes, etc. When Nash makes a growing sculpture this binds him in a moral relationship which can take contractual form when the work is abroad: he has to return at intervals to nurture it.

The Long pieces look mighty in the galleries, whether their constituents are massive or slight. Though they are modest, ascetic even in the material sense, as statements they command attention, and the charge they bring with them comes from this contrast between frugality of the means and the resonance of the result. Nash's gallery pieces are surprisingly soft-spoken, considering their often assertive forms and size. They have made me think of Shaker furniture, neat, wholesome, patient, but they can also be animals, not wild but not entirely domesticated either, their ears pricked for the outdoors. They are less finite than Brancusi's wood objects, less wholly transformed, less taken over. This borderland between taking-and-making and only half taking and letting be cannot be explored in painting and in sculpture made with traditional materials – though one hesitates to say what now counts as traditional sculpture. I recall responding similarly to Caro's works of 1972–74, Veduggio and after, in which the soft, spreading edges of rolled steel hint that this material too has a natural life.

The challenge somehow to overcome or contradict

old materials and methods has left its mark on the paintings of Maurice Cockrill and of William Tillyer. Both have at times broken into the surfaces they were painting on. The signals given are many and contradictory. Violence: Cockrill's way of imagining and painting swings from great vehemence to tenderness, and it must have seemed natural to add breaking the surface of his wood panels to breaking their visual planes with the force of paint. Tillyer's paintings – vehement at the start of the 1980s when he used rough collage and brusque-seeming brushstrokes on a surface that was part canvas, part metal mesh, but now appearing more controlled and free in that Oriental sense where freedom comes from unending contemplation and practice – are clean and broad and often seem to float like the music of Delius; to cut into the board he is working on and combine painted forms with the exactly formed holes, feels like a challenge to painting to justify itself in the face of such violation. Curiosity: if Tillyer's means of expression are primarily membranes of paint stretched across canvases and boards, often on a large scale, what will happen if he breaks that surface – when, like Brecht alienating the spectator in the theatre, he breaks the spell that canvas plus paint work on us, that sense of a special place and encounter? If Cockrill, whose brush can make slashing gestures in strong colours over a scene that could have remained calm and pastoral, physically slashes their surfaces, is he adding a different kind of brushstroke or denying the value of brushstrokes and paint? Reality: like many painters ever since Duchamp attached a bottle brush to his elaborately worked last painting and suggestively call the whole thing *Tu m'*, both Cockrill and Tillyer seek the reality both of the work as made object and of the visual poem they are contriving in their particular ways. For each successful painting there came the moment when these realities were brought into balance and the painter knew his work was done. But in the longer process of developing his art, with whatever degree of conscious or unconscious decision-making, I suspect the painter needs sometimes to throw a spanner into his own works, create a new difficulty and a new opportunity.

Landscape has always been the important concern for both of them, though Cockrill has also made major figure paintings. What it means to each of them is quite different and comes out of distinct experiences. Cockrill was born in Hartlepool but spent much of his childhood in Wales, South Wales and then North Wales, with frequent returns to Hartlepool to visit relatives. Hartlepool meant bomb dereliction and slums. Wales, North and South, meant steel-works. Later he lived in Liverpool. In 1982 he moved to London. Tillyer was born in Middlesbrough, but on the edge of it and facing out, he would stress. From 1960 to 1987 he lived mainly in London, but travelled widely in Britain and abroad. In 1987 he moved into North Yorkshire where he lives and works, when he is not travelling, in something close to isolation.

Their recent paintings appear wholly dissimilar. Cockrill's are full of incident – nature as a turbulent participant in human affairs, joyful and terrible, nature involved rather than observed. After the first impact we learn to read the processes involved, with fluent, broad and reassuring forms meeting staccato incidents, with hard and soft colours and marks. 'Not for him the golden world', Margaret Drabble wrote last year. Certainly not dreams of a paradise lost or to come, but an extraordinary vision in which gold is scattered amid debris and fruitfulness lies with death. His dramatically varied and fragmented life seems to find echoes in the structures of his paintings, but then we must see continuities, the broader reaches of land and sky, as symbolical images of his life too. I think of his involvement in world literature and mythologies, but also in the never-ceasing interplay of daily life, up or down, and common human aspirations. These are continuous, a kind of ground bass. Memory contributes much of his imagery but nostalgia plays no part in it.

Tillyer too paints from memory, but it is recollection of landscape that is his overt subject-matter, and everything else is screened by it. Anything autobiographical, anything like a statement about life will be there only in the guise of expression, the pictorial equivalent of key signature or indication of tempo. The broad sweeps of colour, some more or less even, others broken or mixed, combine qualities of foliage, air and light and are placed with such certainty that they can take on an almost sculptural presence on his white or dark canvases. The image is confident as a whole, yet within it we find dramatic collisions of form. Darkness invades;

light breaks through. He sets positive shapes against negative spaces, but he also plants mighty geometrical forms, man-made forms, among the organic forms of nature. Breaking the surface physically connects with both. His water-colours can be marvellously serene. He obviously cherishes the medium for the transparency and lightness it can deliver, and so do we, remembering Girtin, Cotman and Turner. Yet in the water-colours too we encounter hard forms, collaged on sometimes. His acrylics are really remarkably similar, allowing for scale and an opaque medium, and among his recent ones are those painted on boards into which he has cut geometrical openings, negative shapes that in the latest of them give us glimpses of another painted level behind or beneath. A thoroughly experienced printmaker, in 1990 he was able to bring three-dimensional shapes also into prints, in a series he made in Los Angeles.

'Tillyer's best water-colours are not only good; they are also exceedingly pleasant and attractive', Peter Fuller wrote in 1987, and praised their 'shimmering veils, membranes and pools of pure, vibrating blue'. This is true but only half the truth, because it ignores the toughness of Tillyer's art and his recurring need to confront his own lyricism with hard-edged obstacles. That is how they feel. Of course, the contrast makes for mutual enhancement but only as a by-product of an intentional opposition that comes close to being violent. I read this drama as representing the country/city duality, echoed no doubt by personal conflicts operating in Tillyer as in all of us. What makes his staging of it so important is that, a true dramatist, he is not after a simplistic good/evil, like/dislike opposition. Those geometrical forms have their own dignity and value. It is we (I) who start by seeing them as discordant notes in his visual hymn to natural forces; stay longer, and they become complementary elements. They link Tillyer's landscape painting back to the great classical tradition of Titian and Poussin. This does not mean side-stepping the inheritance of Romanticism: classical landscape painting survived that revolution by adopting disguises that today seem wholly transparent. Turner engaged with it in his early works and never quite turned his back on it; it was central to Corot even when he was painting those fresh, spontaneous-seeming landscapes people see as heralds of Impressionism; it was the core of Cézanne's mature endeavour.

The only one of England's major modern landscape painters who claimed nature as his birthright was Peter Lanyon. Writing not long after Lanyon's accidental death in 1964, at the age of forty-six, Alan Bowness described him as 'a fanatical Cornishman, born in 1918 of Cornish parents in St Ives', who was 'always held in the spell of the remote and mysterious landscape of West Cornwall' where 'land, sea and sky inter-penetrate in a brilliant Atlantic light'. Lanyon's own statements reinforce this: he saw himself as a painter of quite specific natural phenomena, observed and loved by himself, including the clashes of soft and mobile against hard and fixed which characterise Cornwall during all but its quietest days.

Lanyon was no rustic in his experience and thought. Adrian Stokes discovered him, yet this was no Wallis-like primitive he had found, but a middle-class, well-educated young man. Stokes encouraged him to enrol in the Euston Road School in London (where Stokes himself had worked recently), and there Lanyon spent part of 1938. He was taught there a modified form of naturalism based on careful scrutiny of the sitter or other motif; the sub-text, surprisingly, was an essentially urban realism, a realism which took on progressive colouring by opting for man-in-the-street subjects while eschewing Sickert's melodramatics. Back in Cornwall, Lanyon took lessons from Nicholson and was influenced also by Gabo. The result was constructions, but constructions free of their Constructive idiom. Lanyon's artistic persona was already strong, and by the late 1940s he was finding his own voice and means. Cornwall remained his subject, though travels to far-away lands such as Mexico stimulated him, and when he took up gliding as a hobby he found additional experiences of space and movement that he could recreate in his paintings. He had served in the Royal Air Force during the war, in North Africa, Palestine and Italy, but as an aero-engine specialist, not as pilot. In any case, gliding comes close to being the opposite to propelling oneself through the skies at great speed by means of mechanical energy. The glider pilot flies with and thanks to nature, not in contradiction of natural forces, and this is what one encounters also in the best of Lanyon's paintings: nature not idealised, nor paraded as a wild and dangerous beast, but natural nature, unconscious of man though marked with his presence here and there, charged with energies that only to man seem antagonistic or benign.

'My art follows Constable', he wrote in a letter of 1952. One sees what he means, but Cornwall is not Suffolk or Hampstead Heath, and 1950 is not 1820. Lanyon knew a much larger physical world than Constable and was part of an international art world even as he worked in St Ives. Pollock and Abstract Expressionism were part of his context. He was never a son of St Ives only, but had the advantages and the burdens of modern cosmopolitan man. The strength of his art resides precisely in his acceptance of the wider view this, as much as his gliding, gave him and in his insistence on remaining tied to his native land while being alert to the larger world.

It seems we are all 'double men' now: only the true primitive and the urbanite untouched by dreams of nature and without a television set to teach him the facts of natural life can possibly escape that duplicity. To its moral burden we add our ecological guilt and begin to doubt our birthright to anything. So where do we belong after what begins to feel like a second Expulsion?

But it may be that the city will fail. New work processes make for decentralisation. Urban architecture parades its loss of faith. Today we begin to see North American cities, once typical of modernity and still glamorous, as theatres of urban decay and violence. In Adam Smith's day, about the time Wordsworth and Turner were born, America served as a model for the return of man and capital to the land. Perhaps progress will be in such terms in the twenty-second century. Rural life can never again imply isolation and thus we need not lose the 'quickened, multiplied consciousness' (Walter Pater) that is our reward for urban existence. Perhaps the semi-deserted cities will take over from the countryside as centres of peace and William Morris's dream of awakening to quiet and to a smokeless sky – 'I opened my eyes to the sunlight again and looked around me, and cried out among the whispering trees and odorous blossoms, "Trafalgar Square!"' (*News from Nowhere*) – will become reality. In 1890 that dream was sheer regression. Today it seems merely remote. We look to artists for a graspable, energising expression of it; for something like a new landscape in which our urgent need and the longing of Romanticism can meet.

NOTE

The initial stimulus to writing this essay was the fact I came across in Margaret Drabble's *A Writer's Britain* (Thames and Hudson, 1979), that Wordsworth pitied his good friend Coleridge on account of his urban upbringing. I wrote to Ms Drabble to ask for more and she answered most helpfully, directing me to passages in *The Prelude* where Wordsworth refers to this. I have of course made use of many other printed sources for information and commentary. Particularly useful

and/or stimulating were these: Raymond Williams' *The Country and the City* (The Hogarth Press, 1993; first published 1973), Richard Holmes' *Coleridge, Early Visions* (Penguin Books, 1989), Wilfrid Mellers' *Vaughan Williams and the Vision of Albion* (Barrie and Jenkins, 1989), Ann Bermingham's *Landscape and Ideology* (Thames and Hudson, 1987), and Raymond Lister's *Samuel Palmer* (Cambridge University Press, 1987).

They saw more mountains, and the cart creeping over them and among them, small as a stone upon the road. And by and by they got down by a brook and began to travel upward towards the source. There were clear and dark pools in the brook where the trout darted and the man with them said: 'The fish runs away, who knows that man has sinned.' They were among steep woods of oak trees as dense almost as grass, all twisted and grey as if made of stone and very old, but based in greenest leaves and flowers of white, of gold, of golden green. The blackbird sang, and the brook gushed, but they did not speak, except that as they left, the strange man said: 'This is the Castle of Leaves.' Now, there was no longer a path, and the way was over whistling dead grass and grey stones, like ruins of a palace that must have been lofty as the heavens, and when they had gone further still the man said it was 'The Castle of the Wind.' And now the mist washed over all and hid everything but silvered stones and dead grass blades underfoot, and the rain that was like bent grass blades of crystal, through which for a moment a sheep crept up and crept away again, or a hare, grey as the grass, but blackened as if by fire, leaped up and dived into the wind, the mist, and the rain. Stumbling still among the ruins of the wind's castle, they continued to climb, until the rocks, now tall as a man and so dense that some had to be scaled, came to an end at the shore of a lake which they surrounded – 'The Shepherd's Lake.' The cry of a raven repeated at intervals from the same spot

high up above told them that the mountains rose higher yet and in a precipice. The boy sat upon a rock while the two men went out of sight to the other side; his father to bathe, as he had done twenty years before when a young man. The wind hissed as through closed lips and jagged teeth. The mist wavered over the polished ripples of the lake that resembled a broad and level courtyard of glass among the rough hills. The men were silent, and the sounds of their footsteps were caught up and carried away in the wind. The boy was thoughtless and motionless, with a pleasure that was astonished at itself. He could not have told how long he had been staring at nothing over the lake when, at his feet, his father's head was thrust up laughing out of the water, turned with a swirl, and disappeared again into the mist. He had not ceased to try to disentangle that head from the mist when once more he heard that wailing song that used to make his father so glad, and he himself sang back such words as, without knowing their meaning, he remembered; his brain full of the mists, the mountains, the rivers, the fire in the fern, the castles, the knights, the kings and queens, the mountain boys at cricket, the old man with the foxes, the inn dogs lying in the sun . . . the sun . . . the mist . . . his country . . . not the country he had fought for . . . the country he was going to, up and up and over the mountains, now that he was dying . . . now that he was dead.

Edward Thomas

Landscape: terra firma? *Richard Mabey*

William Dawson *View of the Great Chasm of the Axmouth Landslip* 1840

When Edward Thomas enlisted in the Artists' Rifles in 1915, Eleanor Farjeon asked what he thought he was fighting for. 'Literally for this', he replied, picking up a handful of unimpeachably English earth. With hindsight it seems a naive and theatrical gesture. But one knows what he meant: that underpinning our history and values and aspirations is this enduring bedrock – *the* soil, *the* landscape. It is that 'literally' which sounds so misplaced, especially from a poet who had such a scrupulous and sympathetic eye for the details of the physical world.

Yet real landscapes, in all their intricate, mutable, living detail have always been squeezed like balls of clay in the hand. They are distilled for essences, bottled as heritage, reduced to generalities, which are then offered up as 'literal' patches of the real world. The landscapes themselves, not to mention their inhabitants and the cultures they both support, are made poorer and more vulnerable in the process.

The real stuff of landscape can't be pinned down so easily. Not far from the Hampshire chalk hills prowled over by Thomas there is another celebrated landscape – the long stretch of wooded shoreline between Lyme Regis and Axmouth, known universally as the Undercliff. It is a wild and romantic place of ivy-draped rocks and wind-bent ash trees, and the auras left by generations of visiting writers and artists. Jane Austen must have glimpsed it on her visits to Lyme. Tennyson (who once celebrated a more domestic English landscape as the 'haunt of ancient peace . . . all things in order stored') rambled amongst its dark pools and bushy chasms. Most famously it figured as a powerful, liberating backcloth – almost a supporting character in its own right – in John Fowles' novel *The French Lieutenant's Woman*. It is turbulent, as is the way of the Devon coast, but seemingly timeless, and elsewhere Fowles has written of it: 'It looks almost as the world might have been if man had not evolved, so pure, so unspoilt, so untouched it is scarcely credible.'

But in William Dawson's 1840 portrait it has (if you forget the title) an almost pastoral look. Inside the amphitheatre formed by the crumbling chalk cliffs is a wheatfield. Reapers are working through it, and people are picnicking and talking in groups around the edge. A Union Jack is being hoisted above them. It is a rustic scene and unquestionably 'old England'. But its real history is rather different. The events that formed the Undercliff and lay behind Dawson's *View of the Great Chasm of the Axmouth Landslip* are a long way removed from the mythology of a changeless, immemorial landscape. Two centuries ago this was an unexceptional West Country coastline. It was haunted by religious dissenters and the occasional smuggler, and supported a scatter of cultivated fields on top of the cliffs. Then, one night late in 1839, it literally fell apart.

In one sense this was nothing new, as the cliffs along this coast have always been unstable. Water seeps down through the chalk and forms a kind of lubricating layer between it and the harder rocks beneath. Over the centuries small chunks have repeatedly crumbled away. But the landslip of 1839 was a more cataclysmic affair. A huge chalk floe, six hectares in extent, slid off towards the sea, leaving a chasm into which the next section of cliff collapsed. On top was a sizeable wheatfield, already carrying its crop. It fell more or less intact, the right way up, and on August 25th the following year it was ceremonially reaped. The whole event became a source of wonder and foreboding in the district, and more than ten thousand people came to watch the harvest. The reapers were led by young women, who had been given silver brooches in the form of sickles as souvenirs.

More landslips followed and within a few decades the present landscape of the Undercliff began to evolve – a secret wild garden, benignly Gothic on the surface, but underneath an impenetrable and precarious wilderness. Every year the local rescue services are called out for someone who is lost, or has fallen down one of the covered crevices.

The history of the Undercliff is a dramatic one, but in many ways is just an extreme example of the way that change and tradition, natural forces and human labour intertwine in real landscapes. Any country parish will understand that harvest ceremony of 1840 and the ambivalence that seemed to hang over it – the shock giving way to curiosity, the insistence on things going on as usual despite the chaos. These are the traditional rules of human survival in the landscape. Get the upper hand again, if only for a season. Make the best of things. Celebrate the inevitable. Life goes on. Landscapes have always been looked on to bridge the gap between two opposed sets of human needs: for some haven of continuity on one hand, and the vitality of nature on the other; for a familiar environment, fashioned by human hands, and then again for something that transcends the man-made and the artificial.

Myths have abounded in this gap, feeding on its unresolved tensions. Many (as is the way of myths) are mutually contradictory, especially those that cluster around trees and wild woodland, the contrary of civilisation. For example: trees die if they are cut. Trees die if other trees are *not* cut. Woods were planted by men, and must be replanted by them. But 'good' land turns into 'wasteland', unkempt forest, if it is not kept under control.

One of the most powerful myths has been the idea of a national landscape, *the* landscape – some spirit or essence underlying and unifying actual landscapes, which symbolises the British, or more usually English, character. It is of course a rural landscape, despite our having been principally an industrial and urban nation since the late nineteenth century. It was not only Edward Thomas who saw this essential England as being what the First World War was fought for. Rupert Brooke recoiled at the prospect of 'English soil' being desecrated, not long before he became a piece of misplaced English earth himself, interred, as he had prophesied, in the corner of a foreign field. The wheelwright's son and social historian, George Sturt, thought the 'Prussian armies' were 'outraging England in her . . . pleasant cornfields and country lanes'. In letters from the trenches and recruiting propaganda back in the home villages, the notion of what was being defended was repeatedly reduced to a small cluster of familiar rural images: the Downs, stooks glowing in a field at sunset, the call of rooks flying home to a vicarage copse, wild roses in the hedges – a country wholly identified with its countryside.

Similar feelings surfaced in the Second World War, and were tapped by the Ministry of Information in their campaigns to boost morale. And in one celebrated image by Frank Newbould it is possible to see this national landscape outlined in precise detail. 'Your Britain. Fight for it now' runs the caption over a water-colour of what is unmistakably the South Downs. The view is from the top of a hill looking down. In the foreground a shepherd is leading his flock over the open hills, back to a village in the valley. A big, double-chimneyed manor house nestles in a billowing crescent of oak trees. In the distance there are more soaring Downs, a lighthouse and, just glimpsed between the hills, the English Channel, the last ditch between us and the enemy. The picture captures the character of the British landscape of popular mythology, and implies that this was part of all the people's heritage. But in what sense was this true? What exactly did that phrase 'Your Britain' mean? Not the privilege of ownership, of course. Nor that we had a right of access, not even in the 1940s. Nor, for the majority of British town dwellers whose landscapes were being blown apart nightly in the Blitz, did it come close to anything in their direct experience. Its heart, of course, was in the right place, in suggesting that landscape transcends land as property, and does indeed 'belong' to the people, as do the cultural qualities it expresses – fertility, stewardship of the land, peace, space and the shelter of an anciently rooted community. But, as on every occasion when this generalised appeal has been made, the intricate fibre of real landscapes and the lives they encompassed was glossed over. Fifty years on, during which time the character and working life of the Downs had changed dramatically, Newbould's picture was used again, in a campaign by the Council for the Protection of Rural England. The slogan was the same – 'Your Britain. Fight for it now', but this time the enemy, as everyone understood, was closer to home.

What gives a landscape its identity? On the South Downs, local patterns of farming and ownership, and even of vegetation, have repeatedly been transformed. The hills were covered with trees six thousand years ago and almost devoid of them in the seventeenth century. Settlements built in times of plenty vanished during plagues and recessions – or if they happened to spoil the view from the Big House. In prehistoric times small arable fields would have been cleared straight from the wildwood, especially near the foot of the hills. In the medieval period, sheep took over many of the hills, and their grazing produced the classic, flower-rich, short-turfed pasture for which the Downs became famous. But during the Agricultural Revolution of the eighteenth and early nineteenth centuries, much of this was ploughed up for turnips and then wheat – only to revert back to grassland, and then scrub and wood, during the long agricultural depression of the Victorian era. This century the Downs have been cleared and ploughed again, for barley, kale and oil-seed rape. The view from the top of the hill has stayed much the same. But each one of those shifts in the balance between wood, grass, arable crop and human settlement meant dramatic changes in local ecology and social life; and doubtless every one of them was mourned at the time as spelling the end of the old order. Which stage represents the 'true' landscape of the Downs? Who decides? Is our own time – or some hypothetically harmonious Golden Age – the only reference point we can take with respect to a landscape so patently ingrained with history?

Landscape is an old idea but a comparatively new word, and part of the confusion it causes is a consequence of its not having a comfortably settled meaning. The term came originally from the Dutch 'landschap' meaning a region or province, plain and simple. But it entered the English language (as 'landskip' originally) in the seventeenth century as a piece of fashionable artistic jargon, and despite three hundred years of currency in the turbulent world of rural affairs, it has never quite lost that slightly precious air of the salon. Landscape may imply more than the view, but in one kind of usage it is always *out there*, remote and painterly, exterior design on a grand scale. The same could be said of the putative landscape 'designer', who is perhaps seen as a benevolent landowner, or perhaps God, or just occasionally nature itself, as an equally remote force. What is barely even conceived is landscape as a vernacular production, made in a rather haphazard way by us, nature and the weather. Official landscape is the view from the hill, from the top of a horse, through a Claude glass or an aerial photographer's viewfinder.

Yet there is another, more anciently rooted sense of place which has no satisfactory English word to describe it. This is landscape as the home ground, the native patch which becomes familiar by being experienced from ground level, landscape as something you look out *from*, not at. This is way we look at the outside world when we are children, and it can turn ordinary waste patches and favourite trees into whole kingdoms. The poet John Clare wrote unaffectedly of what he called 'pleasant

places', and though, for him, they were intensely personal and local, they make a list with universal appeal:

Old stone pits with veined ivy overhung
Wild crooked brooks o'er which was rudely flung
A rail and plank that bends beneath the tread
Old narrow lanes where trees meet overhead

Yet all such intimate, interior landscapes are set in objective environments of rock, vegetation and climate that change enormously from one corner of Britain to another. Many of these physical features are entirely natural, and seem to permeate the character of different regions however much they have been overlaid or modified by human activity: the stark angles of granite country, for instance, and the softer swells of chalk and limestone; stiff red earth in the Welsh border country, sandstorms in the East Anglian Breckland. Over these regional languages, the intimate local details are inscribed like dialects, and only become intelligible (and often visible) close-to.

Hedges, often regarded as the most defining of all our native landscape features, are a case in point. From a distance they have no identity beyond their functional role as boundaries: they are the grid lines that divide up the fabled English 'checkerboard'. Yet they are hugely varied in age and character: the turf and stone banks – 'reaves' – that separate the narrow Bronze Age fields of Dartmoor; the beech hedges round the windswept edges of Exmoor, and the even taller ones, rooted like mangroves along the banked lanes of Somerset's Blackdown Hills; the hedgerow hollies planted – or simply tolerated – as ploughing guide-posts in East Anglia; the tall, double shelter belts of the Sussex Weald known as 'shaws'; the hedges that are all that is left of whole woods, and which are evocatively known as 'ghosts'.

The intensely local character of these living boundaries is marvellously illustrated by William Cobbett's description of the hedgescape of west Hertfordshire in 1822: 'The custom is in this part . . . to leave a border round the ploughed part of the fields to bear grass and to make hay from, so that, the grass being now made into hay, every corn field has a close mowed grass walk about ten feet wide all round it, between the corn and the hedge. This is most beautiful! The hedges are now full of shepherd's rose, honeysuckles and all sorts of wild flowers; so that you are upon a grass walk, with this most beautiful of all flower gardens and shrubberies on your one hand, and with the corn on the other . . . Talk of pleasure-grounds indeed! What that man ever invented, under the name of pleasure-grounds, can equal these fields in Hertfordshire?' It is not difficult to see why this landscape was so appealing. It had corn and flowers, productivity and decoration. There were more subtle virtues, too: human ingenuity, a tangy sense of place, a frugal use of resources. It was diverse rather than specialised. It made use of the variety thrown up by nature rather than overriding it.

Boundary features like this are usually traced back to deliberate plantings during the heyday of Parliamentary Enclosure in the late eighteenth and nineteenth centuries. In fact most of them are considerably older. Less than a fifth of England was enclosed by Parliamentary Award, and the majority of our hedges are the result of piecemeal enclosures going back as far as the Bronze Age. Many were never planted at all. They began life as strips of natural woodland which were left after a field had been cut out of the forest. Others were the results of shrubs naturally colonising the lines of staked, 'dead' hedges that were features of the landscape even before the Normans arrived. In fact most hedges are a kind of living community that the strict hierarchies of landscape mythology don't care to admit – a symbiosis, a partnership between humans and nature.

So are heathlands, but here the mythology is of a primeval, naturally formed wilderness, which because it hasn't apparently been 'reclaimed' by human work is 'wasteland'. Even Thomas Hardy, whose landscape history was usually impeccable, took this view. His description of Egdon Heath ('A Face on which time makes but little impression' – chapter 1 of *The Return of the Native*) is one of the most evocative passages of landscape writing in the language, yet it still paints Egdon as literally as well as emotionally primordial:

Civilisation was its enemy; and ever since the beginning of vegetation its soil had worn the same antique brown dress, the natural and invariable garment of the particular formation . . . To recline on a stump of thorn in the central valley of Egdon, between afternoon and night, as now, where the eye could reach nothing of the world outside the summits and shoulders of heathland which filled the whole circumference of its glance, and to know that everything around and underneath had been from prehistoric times as unaltered as the stars overhead, gave

ballast to the mind adrift on change, and harassed by the irrepressible New.

Heathland, characterised by sweeps of heather, fine grasses and small shrubs like gorse and broom, is created by the clearance of woodland on poor soils. And it can only be maintained as heath if the cutting, burning or grazing, be it natural or deliberate, is continued. Otherwise it will eventually revert to woodland, as is happening at the moment to many of the unmanaged heaths of southern England. But variations in climate, soil and natural vegetation across Britain mean that this simple regime produces immensely different kinds of heathland: the dry commons of Surrey and Hampshire and the rain-drenched moors of upland Britain; the cliff-top stands of wind-pruned, sun-burned heather on the Lizard peninsula that may be entirely natural, and the fenny heaths of west Norfolk, so pocked with small-scale diggings and glacial scourings that it is futile to draw any line between the natural and man-made. Heathlands, as one modern writer put it, 'represent nature's response' to various human activities. But they are also vulnerable to human activity. The south Dorset heaths that Hardy immortalised as Egdon have been largely destroyed by enclosure and ploughing.

The myth of Parliamentary Enclosure as a creative process, concerned solely with the hedging of the open fields, has been astonishingly persistent. In fact, as well as the Acts which led to the enclosure of four and a half million acres of open field and pasture, there were another 1,893 Acts relating to the clearing and cultivation of more than two million acres of commonland. In almost all instances enclosure involved path-stopping, road-straightening, drainage, the clearance of wood and heath, and a wholesale reorganisation of the geography and economy of the parish.

In this respect Parliamentary Enclosure (despite its strictly local impact) symbolised the processes of centralisation and modernisation that had been gathering pace in the countryside during the 'Age of Improvement'. This is often called the era of 'planned countryside', as distinct from 'ancient' and more organically moulded landscapes. Ancient countryside evolved out of centuries of do-it-yourself enterprise, often involving the whole community. It is asymmetrical and small-scale, and typified by sinuously curving boundary banks, old trees, oddly shaped copses, tapering commons and greens, whose arrangement reflects the natural contours and vegetation. Planned countryside, by contrast, was set out – on a drawing board as often as not – with little sensitivity towards the natural features of the land or the people who lived and worked there. It is uniform and geometric, a tidy patchwork of rectangular fields, symmetrical plantations, straight roads and low hawthorn hedges. As a landscape style it looks much the same in Dorset as in Durham, and everywhere lacks that human scale and quirkiness which makes ancient countryside so appealing.

Tree-planting, ironically, often assisted in this levelling process. Although it could be sensitively done, with indigenous oaks and elms included as part of the new hedgerow planting, it was a central part of the improvement programme, and the trees themselves were sometimes mere ciphers in the grandiose schemes of the improvers. Humphrey Repton had stressed that there was nothing to match tree-planting for those who wanted to display their territorial power, and landowners seemed to agree. The eighteenth and early nineteenth centuries were the heyday of ceremonial avenues, regimented groves and plantations of exotic evergreens. Sir Henry Steuart went as far as to develop elaborate mechanical techniques for transplanting mature trees, to achieve what he called 'the Immediate Command of Wood'. He was an ingenious and intelligent forester, and it would be unfair to call his landscapes 'fakes'; but his book, *The Planters Guide* (1824), gives an extraordinary insight into how trees were viewed by many landowners at the time, as part off-the-peg exterior décor, part arboreal servants who needed disciplining if they were to flourish:

Wood must ever be the grand and effective material of Real Landscape. Over the other materials of picturesque improvement the artist has comparatively little control. With earth he cannot do much; rocks are by far too ponderous for his management; and water can be commanded only in certain situations and circumstances. But Trees or Bushes can be raised any where; and there is no situation so utterly hopeless, as not to be capable of considerable beauty, from wood planted abundantly and luxuriously.

Steuart's 'planting engines' never really caught on. But the ideas to which he gave such extreme expression still prosper. The *imposition* of trees on the landscape, often

regardless of the character of the place and the species of tree, is still widely regarded as a conservation panacea. The flowering cherries which adorn suburban streets across the land are now being planted in increasing numbers in deep countryside. Hybrid Italian poplars are set down along wild river banks, and ornamental American oaks on medieval Chiltern commons. Indigenous trees, that help give local landscapes their distinctive character, are often bulldozed to make way for them, just as they are in commercial plantations.

But even in Henry Steuart's time there were contrary views. In *A Description of the Scenery of the Lakes*, William Wordsworth takes issue both with the idea of an immemorial, changeless landscape, and with the lofty presumptions of the landscape engineers. And his ecologically precise account of the way natural woodland colonises a Lakeland fell, demonstrates his belief that natural landscapes expressed social as well as aesthetic ideals:

From low and sheltered places, vegetation travels upward to the more exposed; and the young plants are protected, and to a certain degree fashioned, by those that have preceded them. The continuous mass of foliage which would thus be produced, is broken by rocks, or by glades or open places, where the browsing of animals has prevented the growth of wood. As vegetation ascends, the winds begin also to bear their part in moulding the forms of trees; but, thus mutually protected, trees, though not of the hardiest kind, are enabled to climb high up the mountains. Gradually, however, by the quality of the ground, and by increasing exposure, a stop is put to their ascent; the hardy trees only are left; those also, by little and little, give way – and a wild and irregular boundary is established, graceful in outline, and never contemplated without some feeling, more or less distinct, of the powers of nature by which it is imposed.

Contrast the liberty that encourages, and the law that limits, this joint work of nature and time, with the disheartening necessities, restrictions and disadvantages, under which the artifical planter must proceed, even he whom long observation and fine feeling have best qualified for the task.

Wordsworth was in no way hostile to humans shaping the landscape. Yet the point he was making about the vitality of nature, and the contribution that this makes to the continuing evolution of landscapes, has been all but dismissed in recent years. The current 'heritage' view of the rural landscape assumes that historical evolution is *over*, that what we now hold, however precariously, is a landscape fully realised. Perhaps one beneficial after-effect of the hurricanes of 1987 and 1990 will be to demonstrate how needlessly defensive and narrow this view is. The storms ruffled old habits of thinking as well as some of the more straitjacketed prospects of southern England, and the extraordinary and unpredictable recuperations that occurred since have been a revelation to many: trees sprouting anew in horizontal or diagonal positions; diminutive vertical meadows blooming on the upturned root plates; forests of unplanted, naturally regenerated saplings shooting through the wreckage.

Yet the ability of landscapes to grow and heal themselves doesn't diminish the contribution which humans can make. The deliberate creation of landscape features, done with respect for the character of a place and the affective bonds which people have with it, almost always enhances its distinctiveness. I am thinking, for example, of the Yorkshire Dales, where the dry-stone walls echo not just the lines and tones of the scree slopes where their raw materials were collected, but subtle changes in the nature of the local rocks – which are reflected again in the 'found-stones' that are gathered to decorate cottage roofs and walls. Or the ancient hollow lanes of the southern counties (where they haven't been frozen by tarmac and nostalgia at some point in the Edwardian era). Two hundred years ago Gilbert White saw them as a *living* record of the life of the village, cut deep into the sandstone rock by 'the traffic of ages, and the fretting of water', and he marvelled at 'their grotesque and wild appearances, from the tangled roots that are twisted among the strata, and from the torrents rushing down their broken sides'.

Oliver Rackham has remarked how 'the countryside records human default as well as design' and some of the richest and most fascinating landscape features can happen more or less by accident. The East Anglian Breckland, a vast inland sandbowl, has for decades been notoriously obscured by immense palls of conifers. But now the Forestry Commission is clearing the first plantings and the ground is inadvertently returning to the wild, sporadically cultivated steppe-land it was in Neolithic times. In northern Britain, many of the lime-rich tips outside derelict chemical factories have turned spontaneously into facsimile chalk downs, covered with sweeps of orchids. The Cumbrian poet Norman Nicholson celebrated similar makeshift landscapes around the worked-out haematite mines near his home, and even saw mining as an essentially 'rural industry', like the harvesting of a root crop.

We are back with John Clare's 'pleasant places' here, those small-scale, distinctive, familiar refuges which perhaps form the best basis for a common understanding of landscape. The view from the hill, so apparently all-including on the surface, has always been the most limited (and limiting) when it comes to meaning. It is appropriative, generalised, and reduces humans (and most other living things) to inanimate props. It is the kind of viewpoint that missed the change of old flowery pastures to chemical-drenched leys, and ancient wood to plantation; that tempts the viewer to look for order rather than liveliness; that neither spots nor cares about the old short cut through a hedge. *Under* the hedge, as it were, both native and stranger can register the real stuff of landscapes, can appreciate their protean diversity, and understand that fossilisation is every bit as deathly as obliteration.

LEISURE

What is this life if, full of care,
We have no time to stand and stare.

No time to stand beneath the boughs
And stare as long as sheep or cows.

No time to see, when woods we pass,
Where squirrels hide their nuts in grass.

No time to see, in broad daylight,
Streams full of stars like skies at night.

No time to turn at Beauty's glance,
And watch her feet, how they can dance.

No time to wait till her mouth can
Enrich that smile her eyes began.

A poor life this if, full of care,
We have no time to stand and stare.

W. H. Davies

Landscape in British music   *David Matthews*

Egdon Heath, Dorset

In Eric Fenby's memoir of the time when he was an amanuensis to Delius, there is a famous account of the blind, paralysed composer dictating to Fenby the opening of his orchestral piece *A Song of Summer*. Delius approaches his task just like any plein-air painter setting up his canvas. 'I want you to imagine', he tells Fenby, 'that we are sitting on the cliffs in the heather overlooking the sea. The sustained chords in the high strings suggest the clear sky, and the stillness and calmness of the scene.' To this he adds a phrase in the cellos and basses 'to suggest the gentle rise and fall of the waves' and a figure on solo flute which 'suggests a seagull gliding by'.

It is a classic musical seascape, similar to others in British music of that period: the opening of Bax's *Tintagel*, or of Frank Bridge's suite *The Sea* (where an oboe replaces Delius's flute). *The Sea* was the first orchestral piece that Britten heard as a boy; in his own words he was 'knocked sideways' by it. Britten of course went on to produce a series of definitive English seascapes in music in his opera *Peter Grimes*, inspired by the sea at Aldeburgh near which he lived for most of his life. The sea in *Peter Grimes* is evoked in all of its moods, from the sullen calm of a grey winter dawn to the sparkling waves on a bright, sunny morning, the moon-reflected glints on the sea at night, or the pent-up violence of a storm.

The evocation of landscape, or seascape, in music, though anticipated in the eighteenth century in such pieces as Vivaldi's *Four Seasons*, began properly as an expression of the Romantic movement, when also the orchestra had developed into an organism sophisticated and precise enough to match the richly coloured palette of the Romantic painter. For landscape music is almost entirely the province of the full symphony orchestra. The landmark pieces – Beethoven's *Pastoral* Symphony, the 'Scène aux champs' from Berlioz's *Symphonie fantastique*, the Wolf's Glen scene from Weber's *Der Freischütz*, Mendelssohn's overture *Fingal's Cave* – date from the same time as the greatest period of British landscape painting. Mendelssohn, who incidentally was a talented water-colourist, made frequent visits to England, where he became a friend of Queen Victoria and her composer husband. But despite the impact he made on British musical life, no outstanding British Romantic music immediately appeared in Mendelssohn's wake. *Fingal's Cave* was less influential than *Elijah*, which must bear much of the responsibility for the dozens of dreary oratorios that British composers were to inflict on their audiences during the next fifty years.

Britain produced no great Romantic composer until Elgar. In spite of its almost wholly German musical background in Schumann, Brahms and Wagner, Elgar's music sounds to us quintessentially English. Here we face an immediate difficulty in trying to define exactly what 'Englishness' in music is. If we link it to the influence of English folksong, then most people might say that Elgar's music does not especially show this, when compared for instance with the music of Vaughan Williams or Holst. Hans Keller, who was able to give an outsider's view, suggested that the folksong influence on Elgar's melodies is just as strong, but is concealed by Elgar's central-European harmonic idiom, so that English listeners do not notice it. But it may be truer to say that rather than being especially influenced by folksong, Elgar created his own folk music as a child: the music he wrote in his childhood was a response, as he himself said, to the first powerful impressions that his native Severn landscape made on him. Elgar's biographer Jerrold Northrop Moore quotes a tune that Elgar wrote at the age of ten during a summer holiday at Broadheath, where he had been born, and from which he had moved when he was two to go and live in Worcester, but which he idealised all his life as a lost paradise. This tune is quite uncannily Elgarian in its contours and its feeling: it has the repeated long plus short note rhythm characteristic of almost all his melodies, and the falling intervals which in later works invariably evoke nostalgia and loss.

Ex. 1

Compare this with the following theme from *Falstaff*, as Elgar described it. 'The march, as we approach the fields and apple-trees, assumes a song-like character:

Ex. 2

until we rest in Shallow's orchard.' It leads to the second of two dream interludes where Falstaff recalls his childhood. In both, Elgar finds a link with the Edenic landscape of his own childhood through the memory of his own folk-theme, Ex. 1. Moore draws attention to many other such places in Elgar's music in his biography.

Passages of graphic 'tone-painting' in Elgar, such as the extraordinary 'malign influence wandering thro' the summer night in the garden' episode in the Second Symphony's opening movement (as Elgar described it to Alice Stuart-Wortley), are quite rare. The essence of Elgar's landscape affinity, like his Englishness, is elusive. It was well expressed by Vaughan Williams when he wrote of Elgar's music that it 'has that peculiar kind of beauty which gives us, his fellow countrymen, a sense of something familiar – the intimate and personal beauty of our own fields and lanes'. Vaughan Williams emphasised that this quality was not found in Elgar's deliberately 'popular' style, 'but at those moments when he seems to have retired into the solitude of his own sanctuary'.

That last phrase might well describe Vaughan Williams's own landscape music, pieces such as *The Lark Ascending* or the Third and Fifth Symphonies where we sense a profound solitary communion with nature. In *The Lark Ascending*, the dialogue between the solitary listener and nature – the lark – becomes, at the end, a monologue for the lark, the solo violin, who leaves the orchestra behind to climb up alone into the clear air. The lark's pentatonic music is a distillation of folksong: unlike Elgar, Vaughan Williams consciously drew folksong into his musical language (he had collected around six hundred folksongs as a young man, together with his friend Gustav Holst). How much more affecting is the bird's pentatonic song than if Vaughan Williams had tried to imitate it more closely, as Messiaen was later to do. The lark's song is made a human song and thus, as Wilfrid Mellers has written, 'by no other composer is the

interdependence of man and Nature more movingly expressed'.

It is hard to say precisely why Vaughan Williams's music should represent the essence of Englishness, as it does for most people. The opening of the Fifth Symphony, for instance, might be *the* archetypal English landscape in sound:

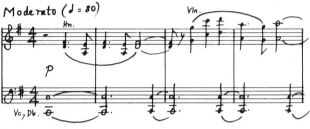

Ex. 3

We can talk loosely of the roundness of the music, of its soft edges; we can point out that the scale on which the music is based is one most characteristic of English folksong – the major scale with flattened seventh. But perhaps all we can accurately say is that Vaughan Williams's understanding of English musical tradition and his love of his native landscape came together, at this particular moment during the Second World War when everything he most cherished was under threat of destruction, to produce this especially resonant sound-image.

Vaughan Williams's Englishness is so deeply rooted that when he takes his inspiration from elsewhere – as in the *Pastoral Symphony* where the inspirational landscape was wartime Flanders – we still feel that it is an essentially English experience that is being communicated. Is the same true of Delius, who lived most of his life outside Britain and who found his most productive inspiration in the mountains of Norway and his own garden at Grez-sur-Loing? Christopher Palmer in his fine book *Delius: Portrait of a Cosmopolitan* has argued persuasively for Delius as 'a true cosmopolitan inasmuch as he celebrates the marvel of the earth *in toto*, he glorifies the sacraments of Nature as she embraces all things and all peoples'. Yet Palmer admits that it is only in this country that Delius's music is really loved, and isn't that because, despite his dislike of England, Delius could not help having an English voice? In *Summer Night on the River*, one of his

Grez pieces and one of the most beautiful of all his works, there is a superficial resemblance to an Impressionist painting in sound. Ex. 4 shows its magical opening (compare Vaughan Williams's Fifth Symphony, Ex. 3, and Ex. 1 and many other Elgar themes: trochaic rhythms would seem to be an especially English feature).

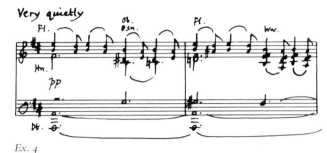

Ex. 4

Palmer compares Delius particularly to Sisley; yet surely there is little real affinity between the Impressionists, with their interest in direct sensation, in capturing the fleeting pleasure of the present moment, and Delius's music which is almost entirely concerned with indirect sensation, with memory, with Elgarian nostalgia for a lost paradise. Again, compare *Summer Night on the River* with Debussy's *Nuages*: Delius and Debussy (whose music is a genuine equivalent of Impressionism) have little in common beneath the surface.

Delius's love of landscape was no passive affair: until syphilis paralysed him in late middle age he was a tremendous walker, spending many summers in Norway walking in the mountains (*The Song of the High Hills*, one of his greatest pieces, is the distillation of these experiences). Gustav Holst throughout most of his life also made long-distance solitary walks in the English countryside, in particular the West Country, which gave him an intimate knowledge of its nature. I want to examine one work in which Holst seems to express the essence of a landscape, the orchestral piece *Egdon Heath*, which he wrote in 1927, towards the end of his life. Holst loved desolate, wild places. In 1926 he read Hardy's *The Return of the Native*, and walked over the stretch of lonely heathland between Wool and Bere Regis that Hardy named 'Egdon Heath'. Holst began writing his *Egdon Heath* the following year, and midway through its composition he called on Hardy, whom he knew well, for lunch, walking to Hardy's house near Dorchester

from Bristol, via the Mendips, Wells and Sherborne. Hardy took him to Egdon and to the hill he called Rainbarrow. The score of *Egdon Heath* is prefaced by a quotation from the first chapter of Hardy's novel: 'a place perfectly accordant with man's nature – neither ghastly, hateful, nor ugly: neither commonplace, unmeaning, nor tame; but, like man, slighted and enduring; and withal singularly colossal and mysterious in its swarthy monotony.'

The overall instrumental colouring of *Egdon Heath* is sombre, and dynamics are restrained: there are only two loud passages. The opening phrase for muted double basses alone has a lonely, weary sound:

Ex. 5

It sets up a pattern of slow, steady movement in even crotchets, like a solitary traveller trudging across the heath's wide expanse (which indeed is the opening image of *The Return of the Native*). The even crotchets are taken up by the rest of the strings. Half of them are muted and half unmuted: muted phrases are answered by unmuted ones, a subtle variation, as if the landscape were alternately being seen in light and in shade. None of the contrasts in *Egdon Heath* are harsh ones, as in the landscape itself with its many different tints of brown and green; and they never disrupt its overall unity. When a new section begins with agitated figures in the strings, like a wind passing over the heath, these are soon steadied by the firm even crotchets on brass and wind. This passage – the first of the work's two climaxes – is succeeded by one of those quiet brass processionals so typical of Holst's music, at the same trudging pace. This is a precise symbol of 'man, slighted and enduring' (the trombone, incidentally, was Holst's own instrument). Towards the end of the piece, flutes and bassoons play a sad, folk-like tune, like a dance of ghosts: it has the same note of poignant regret that Hardy's writing has for 'a time there was . . .when all went well'. The lonely trumpet call at the very end, after the processional has again been glimpsed in the distance, also has a ghostly sound. Even though untamed, the heath, like all English landscapes, is a place of memory.

The composers I have mentioned so far, together with their contemporaries Bax, Bridge, Butterworth (who wrote two exquisite landscape pieces for orchestra before he was killed in the Battle of the Somme at the age of thirty-one), Howells (whose early chamber music is the exception to the rule that landscape music must be for orchestra), Ireland and Moeran, could be thought of as a landscape school in music paralleling the great British landscape painters of a century earlier. The composers of the next generation were neither so especially concerned with nature nor with Englishness. Walton's two orchestral pieces with pictorial inspiration, *Portsmouth Point* and *Scapino*, were based on engravings, by Rowlandson and Callot respectively, of people rather than places. Walton's music is sophisticated, urban, full of sexual passion, and if he has an ideal landscape, it is the Italian one that he adopted as his later home. Tippett, in contrast, is a thorough countryman: he was brought up in rural Suffolk (only forty miles away from Britten) and has never lived in cities. Like Delius, Tippett is a nature mystic (though he is most *un*like Delius as a composer) and pieces such as his *Corelli Fantasia*, the slow movement of his *Concerto for Double String Orchestra* or the 'Ritual Dances' from *The Midsummer Marriage* continue to evoke the English landscape as uncannily as Vaughan Williams or Holst had done. Tippett's music is entirely free from nostalgia: there is no sense of loss, but rather of a vision continually present.

Britten was at the same time the most cosmopolitan of all British composers and the most local. I have already mentioned the huge inspiration of the Aldeburgh seascape, which for many years was the view from his sea-front house. The Suffolk landscape is also a constant, though elusive presence in his music. Perhaps the most explicit landscape music in all Britten's work came at the very end of his life, in his *Suite on English Folk Tunes, 'A time there was'* (Hardy's line, which Britten had set in his *Winter Words*). The suite is dedicated to the memory of Percy Grainger, that great eccentric presence in British music, who had, for instance, collected the folksong 'Brigg Fair' and made his own, ravishing choral setting of

it before presenting it to Delius as the theme for his orchestral variations. It is in the last of the five movements of Britten's suite, 'Lord Melbourne', which includes a complete version of that folksong as Grainger had notated it, that we feel once again that special affinity with the English landscape – and here with all its associations of memory and loss – that Vaughan Williams and Holst had evoked. At the end, the cor anglais, which has 'sung' the folksong throughout, reaches its final phrase as the strings make a cadence into C major, its E flat sounding a bittersweet – and characteristically English – dissonance against the strings' E natural. The words of the folksong here are 'But now to death I must yield'. The phrase is repeated by the clarinet and, inconclusively, by the flute, while the strings prolong their C major chord, quietly fading into darkness. The effect is similar to the end of Mahler's *Das Lied von der Erde*: man lives and dies, but nature is eternal.

Ex. 6

The mood of deep sadness that pervades 'Lord Melbourne' no doubt has much to do with Britten's thoughts on his own impending death, but its elegiac tone is also typical of the way we tend to look at our landscape today. We are constantly reminded that every aspect of the landscape is threatened in some way or other. So sentimentality and nostalgia envelop us: our films and television are pervaded by images of the unspoilt British countryside before the First World War, 'when all was well' (though Hardy did not think so, but looked back to the time of his own childhood). Is it impossible, then, for contemporary artists to celebrate nature as she is, without sentimentality, and without taking refuge in the past? Some, certainly, are showing that it is not. The very fragility of the landscape makes it more precious, and our increasing consciousness of its importance to us, the sustenance it offers to our souls, should help us to cherish it.

In British music today, the influence of the landscape is still strong. Peter Maxwell Davies for instance has chosen to live in one of the wildest and remotest places in Britain, the island of Hoy in Orkney, in order to let its spirit suffuse his music. The result may be heard in such pieces as *Stone Litany* and *Ave Maris Stella*, whose strange, bleak beauty is a mirror of the Orkney landscape. Some of Harrison Birtwistle's music has the rough, gritty grandeur of the Pennine landscape in which he was brought up; though I have never sensed any feeling of *delight* in this landscape, but only its dourness. Robin Holloway, on the other hand, has in his *Seascape and Harvest* recaptured some of the sensual joy in nature that we feel in Bridge or Bax. Holloway has written eloquently of how all aspects of the visual world, from moonlit forests to steel foundries, have affected the substance of his music. Of younger composers, John Casken is especially preoccupied with the landscape of his native Northumbria, as in his orchestral piece *Orion over Farne*; while Judith Weir has returned to folksong, both her own Scots folksong and that of Eastern Europe: her opera *The Vanishing Bridegroom* contains marvellous folk-based evocations of its West Highland setting. Anthony Powers has recently completed an orchestral piece, *Terrain*, inspired by the landscape of his home in the Welsh Marches. He writes: 'My workroom has two windows, one looking west to Wales and the massive escarpment of the Black Mountains, the other east, over England, the Golden Valley and the rich country that rolls to the Malvern Hills on the horizon.' *Terrain* 'tries to encompass this great landscape in its many different moods', and the two kinds of landscape, the one dark, the other light, suggested two contrasted kinds of music, the first harmonic and 'vertical', the second contrapuntal and 'horizontal'.

Writing about music in the descriptive way I have been doing here inevitably leads to some over-simplification. I do not mean to suggest – nor, I am sure, does Anthony Powers – that music can directly depict the landscape in the same way as painting; of course it cannot. It has been argued – for example by Stravinsky – that music is 'about' nothing but itself, and this is certainly true of some purely abstract music, such as Stravinsky's own. But none of the music I have been discussing is of this purely abstract kind; though when it is not intentionally descriptive, as with Vaughan Williams's Fifth Symphony, it becomes difficult, as I have shown, to say why the music seems to evoke what it does, and undoubtedly Vaughan Williams's first concern was with the dialogue between his notes. Music should not really be concerned with direct imitation: Strauss's sheep in *Don Quixote* are very realistic, but most unpoetic, and a musical seascape would not be enhanced by introducing the actual sounds of water. Berlioz makes a useful distinction between musical depiction and musical metaphor, and defines the latter as 'imitation . . . designed to arouse in us by means of sound the notion of the several passions of the heart, and to awaken solely through the sense of hearing the impressions that human beings experience only through the other senses'. It is with metaphor that I have largely been dealing here, and it is the quality of the original emotional response to what has been seen that will determine the choice of the particular musical symbol to represent it. In the best descriptive music the symbolism is precise: could there be a more graphic evocation of a calm sea and grey morning sky than the opening of the 'Dawn' interlude from *Peter Grimes*?

If I end by saying something about my own music, it is only because, as a composer who has been much affected both by landscape and by the visual arts, I can add my own testimony at first hand. The experience of the landscape in all its aspects has always been important to me in the gestation period of a piece, when I too like to go for day-long solitary walks: it is in observing the changing contours of the landscape at walking pace that I find ideas most frequently and productively come. I associate the pace of music with the physical activity of the body, whether running (*Allegro*), walking (*Andante*) or at rest (*Adagio*), so that a piece will often clarify in the mind as I move it through the landscape. This was surely a common association until recently, but most movement in music today seems to relate more to the fast-moving but passive state of the traveller by car, train or plane.

I do not try to *describe* landscape, rather to *invoke* it. The ideas that particular landscapes suggest then develop in their own way, as musical ideas will. Two recent orchestral pieces of mine have been concerned with landscape and with seascape respectively, in different ways. The first, *Chaconne*, deals somewhat obliquely with landscape. The initial inspiration for it was Geoffrey Hill's sequence of poems called *Funeral Music*, a meditation on the Wars of the Roses and in particular on the Battle of Towton, the bloodiest battle of those wars. Hill's evocation of a field after battle, which

> utters its own sound
> Which is like nothing on earth, but is earth

immediately suggested music to me. As I wrote in my programme note, 'a medieval battlefield such as Towton has long since mellowed into the peaceable English landscape, the kind of landscape celebrated by our greatest painters and, in music, by Elgar, Vaughan Williams and Tippett. If that pastoral tradition can no longer be sustained in its innocence, perhaps another might replace it, which reconciles our romanticised sense of a picturesque past with the brutal facts of history'. I did not visit Towton, to see the real battlefield; it was enough that I could imagine it, as a symbolic place. *Chaconne* also contains a dreamlike pastoral interlude, a memory of the tradition I have mentioned, and which was connected in my mind (though not musically) with the dream interludes, and their music of lost innocence, in Elgar's *Falstaff*.

The second piece, *The Music of Dawn*, began when I saw Cecil Collins's painting of that name in the Tate Gallery's retrospective in 1989. It was Collins's last major work, painted in glowing tempera, and shows a priestess standing on the seashore, her right hand pointing down to the sun rising out of the sea. It was enormously suggestive of music, as no doubt it was meant to be, for Collins was the most musical of painters. When I came to write my piece, the painting itself became less important than my own frequent experience of watching the sun rise out of the sea at Deal in Kent. I tried to find musical equivalents for the very gradual changes of light that occur before the sun rises. At each moment there is a subtly different pattern of colours in the sky, yet the shifts of tone are almost imperceptible; and all the time there is the regular, quiet sound of the sea breaking on the shore. The first half of my piece corresponds to this slow process of change: one long, quiet, uneventful paragraph moves smoothly into another; nothing occurs suddenly. The moment of sunrise marks the transition from soft and static music to loud and energetic: the rest of the piece is a dance in celebration of the morning, which was affected both by the sensation of immense power that the risen sun soon projects, and by my seeing another painting by Cecil Collins, his altarpiece in praise of the sun's glory, *Icon of Divine Light*, in Chichester Cathedral.

The sun, the sea, the earth, the sky: we must be very tired of life if we cease altogether to celebrate them. Artists, who have the tremendous gift of being able to translate experience into life-enhancing form, should be the last to despair of our precariously-poised world. Whether composers, poets or painters, we should continue to offer up images of beauty, following as we most appropriately can Ruskin's advice to the painter, to 'go to Nature in all singleness of heart . . . having no other thoughts but how best to penetrate her meaning'.

The greatest delight which the fields and woods minister, is the suggestion of an occult relation between man and vegetable. I am not alone and unacknowledged. They nod to me, and I to them. The waving of the boughs in the storm, is new to me and old. It takes me by surprise, and yet is not unknown. Its effect is like that of a higher thought or a better emotion coming over me, when I deemed I was thinking justly or doing right.

Ralph Waldo Emerson

Every morning was a cheerful invitation to make my life of equal simplicity, and I may say innocence, with Nature herself.

Henry David Thoreau

Gardens where the soul's at ease   *Kathleen Raine**

David Jones *Vexilla Regis* 1948

*In conversation with Martin Gayford

The work of the artist is not to reproduce what everybody sees, but to heal the soul; to remind us, as it were, of our native country – the world of the spirit – and tell us that it is there all the time. Blake says of Wordsworth that what he *thinks* is in nature is not really in nature, it is in the imagination; that is what creates the landscape, not the natural features. Blake also says that 'Nature has no outline, but imagination has. Nature has no tune, but imagination has. Nature has no Supernatural and dissolves; Imagination is eternity'.

The question is whether the artist paints a prosaic description of what we call the external world, or whether the imagination is projected onto it – as you find in the early work of Samuel Palmer, or in David Jones and Stanley Spencer. This is a matter of degree, how much you are projecting an inner landscape, how much you are taking from the outer landscape. But in either case, it is the imagination which works the transformation.

It is the same with poetry. At present there is a fashion for something called poetry but which is in fact journalism or photography – simply a matter of describing the untransmuted everyday commonplace of the world. There's almost a deliberate insistence – I suppose it may be a relic of social realism – that this is all there is. Imaginative poetry like that of Shelley or Keats is scorned because it does not conform to this emphasis on the warts, and the armpits, and the shabby bricks and mortar of the world.

The landscapes of Keats and Shelley, on the other hand, were created by the imagination. Take, for instance, the *Ode to the West Wind* with Shelley's description of the cloud, and the thunder, the locks of the approaching storm. The realist will say, 'How wonderfully he described the lightning!' But Shelley was also interested in inspiration, and the wind of the spirit. There was a wedding of an imaginative landscape – which was really concerned with inspiration, and the Platonic muses, the maenads and so forth – with a natural landscape. Shelley was using the one to communicate the other. That is the meaning of the symbol, which relates always inner meaning and outer correspondence. Modern critics, by entirely eliminating the imaginative dimension, try to reduce Shelley to a poet who was interested in electrical phenomena. By doing so, they leave out the real purpose of the poem.

Keats, with his 'magic casements opening o'er the foam / Of perilous seas and faery lands forlorn' was doing the same thing. This is a purely imagined landscape; there is no such place in nature. Keats wedded it very beautifully to 'Verdurous glooms and winding mossy ways' – which is, of course, an image native to the English landscape, which immediately recalls Samuel Palmer. Indeed, one could describe a typical work by Palmer with those very words. Painting and poetry are both modes of the language of imagination. But we live in an age of the photographic, the realistic – *only* the warts of existence. The imagination has ebbed away – fortunately with some exceptions like Jones, Spencer, Jack Yeats and Cecil Collins.

Cecil Collins didn't go out and paint in the woods; he painted in his studio, and the imagination created the landscape to conform with whatever the communication of the painting was to be. Certain emblems were used – trees in which there is a flow which comes up from rivers below and into mountains beyond. In his work imaginative life circulates very often through a series of objects – rocks, river, trees, birds – the flow of the one life going through them all. But there's nothing naturalistic in it: it's a kind of archetypal landscape, a world created by the imagination of the painter.

One sees a painting of his and at once one thinks, 'Ah yes, that's Collinsland.' You step into it immediately, and recognise it. Either you feel 'Home at last!' – which is what I feel – or, like some people, you feel 'There's nothing like this in the world; it's not real'. I remember someone saying to Cecil of one of his paintings, 'There's no such place'. He replied, 'Well, there is *now*' – he himself had created that place which henceforth we can all enter and inhabit.

Of course, there has to be a correspondence between the archetype and the outer world. In this connection one thinks of Henri Corbin's definition of the imaginal world – *l'imaginal*, as against *l'imaginaire*. His point being that whereas the imaginary is not real, the imaginal *is* the reality within, the soul's reality. He describes it as an inter-world between inner and outer, in which ideas are given form, and in which sense-impressions are given meaning – as in Palmer, where some rural scene becomes informed with feeling and imaginative reality. There's always that meeting. In some cases it is more on the one side, in some more on the other. In Collins, it is almost all from within, with a minimal assimilation of natural appearances. But, sometimes, in the case of a fairly ordinary Victorian landscape painting, one feels, 'The painter *saw* something, something got into that picture'. Turner did this seemingly with no effort at all; in his paintings of many different places there is continually this interplay between inner and outer.

Even so, with all Victorians – even Palmer – I feel there was a load of ash, as it were, poured on their imaginations by the increasing materialism of the age. With the Impressionists again there was a coming to life, particularly with Monet – a meeting of inner and outer. It's true that if you go to Etretat, or Argenteuil, the shimmering light is really there. But then, what is the difference between inner and outer? By the late nineteenth century, the Newtonian idea of the solidity of the outer world – reality being what is outside us – had begun to break down. It is really a heresy: even to modern physiology what appears to us as an outer object is recognised in fact as an experience of sensation. What you see out of the window is really in your mind. At that time it was beginning to occur to painters – Turner to an extent, Monet certainly – that you couldn't draw a hard and fast line between 'objective' reality and the mind that experiences that reality.

Plotinus said that nature is a projection from the soul, which in order to contemplate itself, has to be externalised – which comes quite close to the Indian metaphysical idea of the external world being a *maya*, simply a flow of appearances in the mind. The mind to which they appear is the living reality. Whereas the West has tended to believe that the thing outside is 'reality', and mind merely a passive recipient. The truth, of course, is that there is a very subtle interplay between inner and outer, and now in the twentieth century we are once more aware of it. We can no longer be so naive about the solidity of objects.

Van Gogh, in painting his chair as he did, was imbuing it with quality, not just existence. Those kitchen scenes by Vermeer which are kindled with the light of love have also some of that light which Van Gogh painted. One cannot call something a work of art, surely, unless it is – in one way or another – depicting the landscape of the soul: a living landscape, not an 'objective' report like a news bulletin on a television screen.

In the paintings of northern India – I remember Ben Nicholson was very keen on them – there are very beautiful landscapes in which every tree, and every leaf of every tree, every petal of every blossom is perfect and entirely imaginary. The colours – brilliant oranges and blues – are not naturalistic. The whole is an imaginary landscape, a mythological or imagined world. The Chinese landscape painters are different. They speak of the transience, and the great space of the void out of which things open and into which they vanish. You move freely in this evanescent landscape; things lose their obsessive solidity. There is a recreation of rock shapes, of rivers, and waters and boats, but given a totally different dimension by a strongly Buddhist vision of appearances, which, through their very transience, have an epiphanic beauty. All the time, there is this flow of appearances; as in a Japanese haiku, suddenly a frog emerges from a pond and then it's gone again. Each moment brings some wonderful spectacle of nature before our eyes, and takes it away again. Surely the Chinese are the greatest landscape painters of all.

For the Western mind, on the other hand, landscape is generally a solid thing. You expect to find it the next day and the next year, for ever and ever – which is of course completely wrong. Stanley Spencer once said something very revealing to me. 'Looking at one of my old paintings', he remarked, 'I've often thought, "That's absolutely the spirit of Cookham; I must go and look at that place again". But it's never there: the place that you painted, you can never find again.' Cookham wasn't just somewhere you could find in the street. His own life was woven into it; in other words, it was a place of the imagination. Or, quite simply, he loved it. Love is the secret, although the form that love takes is not the same in the case of every painter.

David Jones's Wales, of course, was also a place of the imagination. In his painting *Y Cyfarchiad i Fair* (1963), the Virgin Mary is surrounded by a foxglove, ponies, birds, low stone walls, and other things which are emblems of Wales. In other words, he has put her in an imaginary place, and built Wales around her from memories. When he painted in Capel-y-ffin, he very often also put in those little ponies to which he attached great importance because he thought they were descended from the Roman cavalry. David would never put anything in a painting without its having an emblematic dimension – sometimes almost too much so. He wouldn't just copy nature. His art had to speak of history and the Catholic faith, the things that he cared about. That is how an artist works. Experience must be reshaped in the imagination before it becomes a painting.

I remember his saying once that it's very difficult to get everything in a picture up to the same height and degree of imaginative transmutation. For example, take cows. You somehow have to inform them with an intensity and a realisation of meaning equal to the more highly important parts of the painting. It's a matter of enhancing everything.

In order for him to paint it, a place had to have resonance, to be connected with the things he cared about – Romano-British history, the Catholic faith, the First World War. I remember staying with Helen Sutherland at Cockley Moor over Ullswater in the Lake District when David was staying there too – she had bought many of his paintings and he visited her often. It was within sight of High Street, the furthest point to which the Romans had occupied the land, and David clung to this straw – that here the Romans had at least been. But he didn't enjoy painting that landscape, it never entirely worked.

He did, on the other hand, paint some very beautiful paintings when Helen Sutherland was living at Rock Hall in Northumberland. There was a little church there of which Helen was very fond. David entitled a painting he made of it *The Chapel Perilous*. That is to say, in order to paint it, he had to invest it imaginatively. It wasn't actually in Wales, but at least it was in a Welsh epic – because he had put it there. The Christian theme also enabled him to embody this place in his imaginative world. But it had to be either Wales – the Wales of the imagination, that is – or some equivalent to become part of the imaginative country he was painting. He couldn't paint just how things looked. Neither was Wordsworth's Lake District – the place that Wordsworth saw in *his* imagination – of any interest to David at all. It gave him no straw to cling to; it had to be this particular Welsh universe.

In the very beautiful Irish landscapes of Jack Yeats, again, the imagination finds its home in a certain place and light. His works are infused with the Celtic vision,

the Celtic twilight, of which his brother speaks. Forms become elusive, shapes shift constantly; they are not hard, affirming themselves, but all the time changing. David Jones loved those changing shapes and lights of the Celtic imagination – transparent, subtle – he wrote about them very beautifully. Jack Yeats had that quality too, although his colours are very different and more vivid.

Why did Samuel Palmer love the Vale of Shoreham so much? His father bought a house there, and I suppose to a young Londoner suddenly the country became accessible. It was a tremendous adolescent excitement; and of course it was also Palmer's discovery of Blake. Everything happened at once. Again, Palmer's early work is a transposition into an imaginative world. As Brian Keeble[1] has pointed out, in some of the paintings there are pieces that are clearly taken from Shoreham, but also one finds, for instance, palm trees, things that are not at all part of Shoreham, but belong to an imagined Holy Land. Poor Palmer, when later he began to paint very meticulous oil paintings of nature to make money, he lost all that. The wonderful Palmers are those in which he was painting a landscape of the imagination; happily rediscovered somewhat in his wonderful engravings of Milton and other late works.

Being born into this world immediately presents us with an objective correlative to the imagination. In childhood, as Wordsworth said, this is very strong. But other painters have come to it later. For a painter like David Bomberg, coming out of the First World War and finding that you were still living must have been like coming back to life after death. I suppose the earth presented itself in that new-born way that presumably it did to Palmer when he went to Shoreham. Some experience of marriage between the inner and the outer seems to take place before a painter can really paint a landscape. It's like falling in love – indeed it is precisely that – and at any time in life one can fall in love. People, not just painters, find their landscape of the heart in many different places – some in the wonderful landscapes of Italy and the Mediterranean, the olive-groves, the vines, the terraced hills, the palimpsest of man on nature. Others – Yeats, David Jones – in the twilit Celtic world. Nicholas Roerich found his imaginative world in the Himalayas. Those peaks are still the habitations of the Lord Shiva and the gods of India; that is to say of the

Indian imagination. Something of the sort must be true of every inspired artist.

Sadly, few now have this imaginative vision. Anyone who can't see that something terrible has gone wrong in much of the art being produced in our lifetime just hasn't used their wits. Beauty is a word which has dropped out of modern criticism, whether of art or of poetry. It is regarded as something trivial, like a 'Page Three' girl. Whereas, of course, to the Platonic tradition – and all the artists I have been discussing could be put within the Platonic context – it is the most profound expression of inner reality that there can be. Beauty is an expression of the soul's vision of its own highest reality. But in a great deal of modern painting you don't find it at all; it's almost deliberately cancelled out, as if to say: this is not true. If any beauty comes into a work, that work immediately falls under suspicion.

Much work of our own time is consciously the reverse of beautiful. Francis Bacon was an important painter, perhaps a great painter – but he deliberately excluded beauty from his work. He was a charming man, highly intelligent (curiously enough his favourite poet was Yeats); there's no question of his total dedication and sincerity; he was a completely committed painter, and there's no pretence, fudging, or lying about his work: in that respect, it's impressive. It's a reflection of the experience that our Western world has undergone as a result of the breakdown of our civilisation. But art should reflect the reality of man, of what we are. Bacon's art is a true expression of the view that life is utterly meaningless. And that, in another sense, is *untrue*.

Art, like landscape, should heal. As I said, when I first saw paintings by Cecil Collins, I thought 'Ah, home at last!' – the world of the soul, the world which is alive, which has meaning. As Yeats wrote of 'Palmer and Calvert, Blake and Claude' and their 'Gardens where the soul's at ease'. We're always looking for the Garden of Eden, and, of course, this earth truly is the Garden of Eden if properly seen. Our age has largely lost that vision – but the painter's task is to see and communicate it. Palmer saw it, and Turner, David Jones, Jack Yeats, Stanley Spencer, the painters of northern India and China. They remind us, saying, 'Look, it's here all the time'.

NOTE
1   Brian Keeble, 'The Soul's Infabulous Alchemy: Samuel Palmer's Vision of Nature', *Temenos* 13, 1992.

After a good deal of wandering about, I came upon two very remarkable passages of country situated in the arms of land which embrace the great area of St Bride's Bay . . .

In this direction, nearer the sea, the earth is comparatively flat, but this flatness is deceiving and makes the discovery of little steep valleys more surprising. These valleys possess a bud-like intricacy of form and contain streams, often of indescribable beauty, which run to the sea. The astonishing fertility of [these] valleys and the complexity of the roads running through them is a delight to the eye. The roads form strong and mysterious arabesques as they rise in terraces, in sight, hidden, turning and splitting as they finally disappear into the sky. To see a solitary human figure descending such a road at the solemn moment of sunset is to realise the enveloping quality of the earth which can create, as it does here, a mysterious space limit, a womb-like enclosure – which gives the human form an extraordinary focus and significance.

It was in this country that I began to learn painting. It seemed impossible here for me to sit down and make finished paintings 'from nature'. Indeed, there were no 'ready made' subjects to paint. The spaces and concentrations of this clearly constructed land were stuff for storing in the mind. Their essence was intellectual and emotional, if I may say so. I found that I could express what I felt only by paraphrasing what I saw. Moreover, such country did not seem to make man appear little as does some country of the grander sort. I felt just as much part of the earth as my features were part of me. I did not feel that my imagination was in conflict with the real, but that reality was a dispersed and disintegrated form of imagination.

At first, I attempted to make pictures on the spot. But I soon gave this up. It became my habit to walk through, and soak myself in the country. At times I would make small sketches of ideas on the backs of envelopes and in a small sketch book, or I would make drawings from nature of forms which interested me and which I might otherwise forget. The latter practice helped to nourish my ideas and to keep me on good terms with nature. Sometimes, through sheer laziness, I would lie down on the warm shore until my eye, becoming riveted to some sea-eroded rocks, would notice that they were precisely reproducing in miniature the forms of the inland hills. At all events, I never forced myself here, or consciously looked for subjects. I found it better to visit the country because I liked it – and ideas seemed to come gradually and naturally.

Graham Sutherland

The British landscape tradition   *William Vaughan*

Paul Nash *Pillar and Moon* 1932-42

LANDSCAPE AND ENGLISHNESS

Painting landscapes is something that artists in this country have been particularly good at over the last two centuries. So much so, in fact, that the practice has come to be talked about as being essentially 'British', or, to be more truthful about the matter, 'English'. It has taken its place alongside other national institutions, such as pubs and parish churches, afternoon tea and Savile Row suits.

At first sight, there may seem to be little harm in this. After all, haven't these artists largely been depicting native scenery. And what is wrong with a little pride in a national achievement?

At second sight, however, the habit might not seem so innocent. For what might seem to be a little disingenuous boastfulness can easily become a form of restriction. This limitation can affect both the practice of artists and our own perceptions about this country.

The limitation that the concept can provide for artists can be deduced from the most famous book that deals with the question of Englishness in British art. This is, of course, Nikolaus Pevsner's study, *The Englishness of English Art*. This book is important in many ways. It looked at art produced in this country in a positive light, and suggested that we had more to be proud of than we might think. But ultimately it implied that the defining characteristic of such art was its 'Englishness'. And this quality often interfered, Pevsner suggested, with artists of this country achieving the highest rank. In particular he felt that Englishness had little to do with the modern world, and that artists working in this country in this century must be doomed by their very national character to remain in the second rank.

The romantic topography of Christopher Wood and then Mr. John Piper, Eric Ravilious, and some others may delight us as specifically English, but I doubt whether in a future display of twentieth-century painting the English will be among the principal contributors.[1]

Pevsner wrote in the 1950s, when many critics thought that modernist art was the only type that could be considered seriously. It occupied the high ground of taste. Like the greatest art of the past, it reached beyond place and period. It was international, universal. National art, by contrast, was limited to local interest. You had to have a soft spot for 'Englishness' – as Pevsner did – to appreciate what was good about the art of this country. Forty years later we have a different view, and it may seem that this is a cue for the 'outmoded' Romantic nature of English landscape art that Pevsner identified (and liked so much) to be reassessed. Over the past decade, as representational and semi-representational art has returned to favour, we have seen British art of the twentieth century being talked about with a new bullishness. Certainly this has in some senses been justified. It has allowed space for a reassessment of the work of many artists – including such major figures as David Bomberg and Lucien Freud. But it is also something we must be careful about. We do not want to substitute one straitjacket for another – to replace modernism with parochialism. We should not seek to fetter painters to a tradition – particularly to a tradition that has associations that could be damaging to our own perception of the actualities of the world we live in.

This brings me to the other limitation: the limitation for us as spectators and consumers of art. For by emphasising national characteristics in works created in Britain we run the risk not only of parochialism, but also of anachronism. We could be perpetuating a stereotype that was created in a very different age, and for very different purposes. Most of the current apparatus of our national image was forged in the eighteenth and nineteenth centuries, when Britain was expanding as an industrial and imperial power. As Linda Colley has shown recently,[2] the image of 'Britain' as a national identity – as opposed to a broad geographical definition for a group of islands off the coast of Europe – was purposefully manufactured in the eighteenth century to give coherence and thrust to the new amalgam of nations created by the Act of Union between England and Scotland in 1707. Within this Union the English always had the upper hand, and it is undoubtedly for this reason that 'Englishness' became the principal strand in the cultural image of the new conglomerate. I have argued elsewhere[3] that this also became the leading factor in the characterisation of a national school of art.

In the early nineteenth century – when there was first talk of there being a 'British School' of art – the art of the country became defined in terms of a rampant naturalism. This naturalism was held to represent all that was best about the British spirit. It was seen to come from the same spirit of individualistic enterprise as had fuelled our embrace of Protestantism, of empirical scientific research, of commercial and industrial expansion, of colonial conquest. It was, in a word, that image of progressive Protestantism that has so frequently been seen as the principal engine of the development of western capitalism.

By the Victorian period this image had taken on a decidedly racist aspect, with the Germano-Nordic English and lowland Scots representing a progressive grouping to be set against the 'backward' Celts in Wales, Scotland and Ireland and the 'primitive' or 'degenerate' non-European nations that were in thrall to British Imperial power throughout the world. This is the argument mounted by John Ruskin, the leading art critic of the age, in his essay *The Two Paths* of 1858. In this he asserts that all progressive nations have a culture based on nature and all degenerate ones a culture based on decorative or formal elements. In the former category he placed the English and the Scots. In the latter he put the Indians and the Irish. He cites the decorativeness of Indian fabrics and Celtic manuscripts to prove his point about the innate degeneracy of the societies that produced them. Ruskin was writing at a time when the English had been rocked by the bloody events of the Indian 'Mutiny' of 1857, and were equally disturbed by the growing signs of resistance to British rule in Ireland. While not excusing what he said, one can at least gain an idea of why he said it. But for us to perpetuate some of the myths about 'Englishness' that were forged at this time and in these circumstances would be a different matter.

I do not wish to suggest for a moment that anyone supporting the 'English tradition' in art these days would share the assertions made by Ruskin in *The Two Paths*. Nor is support for 'Englishness' necessarily a sign that one is doing so. Apart from anything else, 'Englishness' has taken on a softer, cosier aspect in the period of British decline in the twentieth century. Yet, like the far from cosy King Lear, it still expects much of the old deference, even after having relinquished so much of its power. And a surprising number of us are still prepared to play Cordelia to it and give it that respect. The very fact that so many of us (myself included) still frequently interchange the words 'English' and 'British' as though there were no real difference between them is a symptom of this. In our multicultural, post-imperial society it is an extraordinary thing to do.

Both because it deals so much with the depiction of the scenery of the British Isles, and because it is so frequently involved with the issue of naturalism, landscape painting has been particularly prone to being seen as an exemplification of Englishness. This is, I think, a shame, as it limits the understanding of a rich and varied practice.

In reviewing developments in landscape painting in Britain over the last two centuries, I want to look at how landscape painting as a practice became established in this country, and how it was developed and continued. But I want as well to consider how the image of a national art form developed, and the ways in which this affected the practice of landscape. Finally I want to see how artists have negotiated the dual traditions of a professional practice and a national stereotype. I hope to be able to show that the strongest artists have exploited the resources of a tradition in ways that are useful to them, rather than falling under its thrall. Ultimately, whatever it is that is best about the landscape art produced in this country over the last two centuries, it has to be something more than the celebration of a fictive national identity.

BRITISH LANDSCAPE BEFORE THE TRADITION

It was only in the nineteenth century that critics began to talk about a national tradition of landscape painting. In the eighteenth century things looked very different. At that time British artists had virtually no reputation at all. Their concern was to show that they could match the work of those continental artists who dominated the art market and received the most powerful patronage. The taste for landscape at that time was set by the major patrons, aristocrats like Lord Burlington who had made the Grand Tour to Italy and admired the classical landscape of seventeenth-century French and Italian artists like Claude, Salvator Rosa and Poussin. These people looked to landscape to provide images of Arcadia – images that were also reflected in the 'landscape' gardens that they had constructed on their estates. Their visual sense of ideal scenery was enriched by their knowledge of classical literature, by the poetry of Virgil and Ovid, and by those British poets from Spenser to Thomson who had celebrated nature in imitation of the classical pastoral.

As well as this classical form of ideal landscape, there was as well an alternative tradition. This was that of the careful delineation of 'local' nature represented by the Netherlandish naturalists of the seventeenth century. Dutch and Flemish art was much in evidence in Britain. It had its place in the nobleman's cabinet as a foil to the 'ideal' art of Italy. In more modest households it predominated. Such art was cheap, and readily available. Britain's developing economy had already made it one of the principal centres for the sale of art by 1700, and Netherlandish painting was one of the staple commodities to be found in the auction houses. Much of this was imported. But many Dutch and Flemish artists had come to settle in Britain, particularly in the latter part of the seventeenth century when the Dutch economy began to go into decline.

It has long been recognised that the practice of painting in this country was transformed at this time through the example of Dutch artists and their Flemish neighbours. Often there was a direct line on contact through apprenticeship. The early sporting and landscape painter John Wootton, for example, was a pupil of Jan Wyck. Because it was so widespread, too, Netherlandish art tended to reach beyond fashionable circles to the provinces. When he was a young man in Sudbury, Suffolk, in the 1740s, Gainsborough formed his first manner through copying Dutch art, particularly the work of Ruysdael. Later he was to call this his 'schoolboy stile'.

But, as Gainsborough's slightly disparaging term suggests, there was also a feeling that Netherlandish art was not enough. It was 'mere' naturalism that could not compete with the higher ideals of classical art.

The first British artist to demonstrate a clear competence in handling classical landscape was the Welshman Richard Wilson. Perhaps it is for this reason that he was so often referred to in the nineteenth century as the 'father' of English landscape. He was revered as having given an 'intellectual' dimension to a practice that had been seen before as a matter of mere copying. Constable once envisaged him walking in Elysium 'arm in arm' with Milton and Linnaeus; thus making it clear that a true landscape painter was the equal of the poet and the scientist. For contemporaries Wilson's main credentials lay in the fact that he had studied in Rome – the home of ideal art. The backbone of his career came from his ability to paint classical subjects and depict views with a grandeur that suggest the work of Claude and Poussin. Yet it must be added that Wilson was too good a painter simply to produce pastiches of classical landscape. He had a unique feeling for atmospherics, and gave a melancholic tinge to his views that suggests a thoroughly eighteenth-century sensibility for the passage of time.

Wilson brought the classical landscape back home in more ways than one. For he also painted views of native British scenery using the pictorial rhetoric he had acquired in Rome. Such scenes also suggest a new and important scope for British landscape painters. In the later eighteenth century it became increasingly the habit for the gentry and middle classes to make tours of their native countryside. This habit began, no doubt, in imitation of the Grand Tour to Italy that the greatest of the noblemen had been in the habit of taking since the seventeenth century to complete their education. The development of the British tour marked the spread of wealth and leisure to a wider segment of society. But such people, if not yet able to indulge in the time and expense of a visit to Italy (this was a boon that came to them in the nineteenth century), could at least expect some enlightenment and instruction while exploring their native countryside. By clothing local scenery with classical grandeur Wilson could suggest that the appreciation of natural beauty could be available even to those who had not had the privilege of going to the Roman Campagna.

Wilson was not alone in suggesting this. There were by this time plenty of other painters and theorists to give it credence. In the 1770s this led to the development of the theory of the 'picturesque'. The picturesque – literally meaning looking 'like a picture' – was a quality that the discerning could find in nature if they looked at her in the right way. Its principal early promoter was the Reverend William Gilpin, an amateur artist who went round the country taking views of celebrated sights and altering them to fit in with his 'picturesque' principles. His first tour – of the River Wye – was made in 1769. A few years later he published this as a guidebook –

complete with illustrations. The book sold prodigiously. Gilpin was but the first of an army of such picturesque tourists and tour guides.

It is hard to exaggerate the importance of the taste for the picturesque in developing the depiction of native scenery. For where the tourist went, the artist was soon to follow. Sandby, Cozens, Pars, Skelton, Hearne, Malton, Towne . . . there is a seemingly endless list of painters who provided views for this market in the late eighteenth century. This was the business that Turner first worked in as a young water-colourist in the 1790s. Along with Thomas Girtin and John Sell Cotman, he was one of those who showed that this taste could be developed into a new and more intimate kind of sensibility.

The taste for the picturesque brought with it a wider aesthetic appreciation, in which local and antiquarian interests had a place beside ideal beauty. Yet it was not the only way in which taste was diversifying at this point. Equally important – more so, some might argue in fact – was the development of that penchant for sensational effects that came to be described by the word sublime. Nothing indicates a change in ideas as much as a word gaining a new meaning. Before the eighteenth century 'sublime' had meant a superior kind of beauty. Now it came to mean that which was overpowering, terrifying and frightening. This was a change that was brought about, as much as anything, by the essay on the Sublime and Beautiful by the philosopher and statesman Edmund Burke.[4] Burke's argument, in a nutshell, was that our sense of beauty was stimulated by that which we found attractive, and our sense of the sublime by that which we found frightening. The sublime was our aesthetic response to that which was overpowering, beyond our reach or comprehension. Whatever the shortcomings of this view, it has been immensely influential. In the late eighteenth century in particular it seemed to provide the rationale for a whole aesthetic of terror, the representation of the wild, bizarre, and strange that could be found in all forms of art. Doubtless this taste for 'sublime' themes in the new sense of the word related to that fundamental shift of perception that is associated with Romanticism. This is the shift that led to the rejection of the idea that reason alone was sufficient to account for our nature and to provide us with ways of

controlling nature, and to the understanding that nature was a mysterious and unknowable area and that our control on events and our own destiny was always a tenuous matter. Such feelings – which must occur to any thoughtful person in any age – took on a special poignancy in the later eighteenth century because it was so clear that rapid changes were taking place for which there were few explanations. These can be symbolised for us nowadays by the great economic upheaval that we call the Industrial Revolution and by the huge social and political changes of the time of the French Revolution of 1789.

Equally striking in the later eighteenth century was the desire to confront these changes, rather than to hide from them. This is perhaps why, in the end, the concept of the sublime was so important. It gave a space in aesthetic contemplation to accommodate the frightening and unknown. Sometimes it was to lead to a ghoulish tickling of the fancy – as in the Gothic novel or in the eccentricities of a painter like Henry Fuseli. At others it was to lead to the stimulus for action – as in the heroic history paintings of David – or to the profound questioning of human nature – as in the work of Goya. In landscape painting it led to the taste for the portrayal of wild mountainous scenes, often with some image of humans being crushed by the events of nature. As with the taste for ideal beauty and for the picturesque there were precedents found. The most important in landscape were the fantastic pictures of the seventeenth-century artist Salvator Rosa. Appropriately, the taste for sublime landscape came in the first place from Rome, and was very much an international affair. The painter Claude-Joseph Vernet was the first to make a name for his 'sublime' scenes of wild mountains, storms and shipwrecks. Richard Wilson – who had known Vernet in Rome – attempted the genre in England. But by far the most successful painter in England to exercise the genre was the Alsatian artist Philippe Jacques de Loutherbourg, who came to settle in England in 1760 and had a highly successful career.

Nowadays, when we look at de Loutherbourg's sublime fantasies we might find them a little over-theatrical – too full of dramatic effect. In fact he was as well a theatre scene painter and was important in bringing a new degree of illusionism to that art. But then we are looking at him from a period when the mimetic image has become a commonplace – easily reproduced mechanically through photography. For de Loutherbourg's generation such illusionism could be admired as sheer wonderment. De Loutherbourg also had the misfortune to be followed by Turner, who rivalled him in sensationalism and re-presented such effects in terms of a more original engagement with the experience of paint.

We should not leave this subject without reminding ourselves of the importance of theatre and display for the development of landscape painting at this time. The late eighteenth century was the time when illusionistic scene painting came into the theatre – itself a sign of a growing taste for sensationalism. Many of the leading landscape painters of the period worked for the theatre as scene painters. De Loutherbourg himself innovated the idea of a theatrical landscape show, which he called the 'Eidophusikon'. There were other types of scenic illusionist display that followed – in particular the panorama and the diorama. It also became the habit to endow traditional landscape paintings with the drama of theatrical display – as did the painter John Martin. Such sensationalism attracted a wide audience and allowed landscape to enjoy a popular world well beyond the confines of high society and the academy. It also had its impact on the shape of 'high' landscape. Where do the broad panoramic vistas in Turner's work come from if not from the theatrical landscape of his time? Eventually such displays were to prepare the ground for the illusionism and wonder of the cinematic spectacular.

I am drawing attention to this tradition here, because I want to make clear that in the Romantic period there were new dimensions set up for landscape. The representation of nature became important for the understanding of human fate and experience in a way that it had not been before. It was not just 'out there' it was also 'in here', inside the spectator. This, ultimately, was the true significance of landscape. Earlier in the century the philosopher Jean-Jacques Rousseau had given civilised man a persuasive image of what he had lost by straying from his original state of being. The contemplation of nature became a way of re-evoking this primal condition. It was the mirror that man could hold up to himself, to perceive his inner world.

Not all landscape artists were playing for such high stakes. Some preferred to be reassuring, giving people images of worlds they would like to live in, or trying to reassure themselves that nature was at heart a friendly, pleasant place, created by divine providence for the benefit of man. But even here there was a sense of loss. For all landscape painting was addressing an urban society that was feeling an increasing distance between itself and the natural world. It involved a kind of yearning – be it for a paradise lost in the past or locked up in man's unconscious.

While these new tastes in landscape came into being in the period after 1760, it was the events following the French Revolution that first stimulated a concept of them as part of a national landscape. On the one hand the reaction against the 'unnatural' events in France led to a valuing of the British countryside as a symbol of all that was normal and healthy. This was the beginning of the idea of the 'rural' idyll not just as a sentimental memory – as it is in the work of Gainsborough in his last period – but as a vivid reality. The rustic scenes of George Morland first brought this in in the 1790s, and in the period after 1800 there is a whole school of artists dedicated to the vivid and 'real' portrayal of the countryside. This is really the background of much local painting – for example that carried out in Norwich by John Crome and his followers. We should be careful, too, in seeing this simply as an expression of local pride. For in Britain such 'local' painters were also addressing the urban society of the big metropolis, in particular London, where the major exhibitions were held. Most of the rural painting carried out at this time was essentially for an urban society, and was made to satisfy a feeling for the reality of the English countryside. Almost all the painters who espoused the cause of naturalism at this time, and went forth to seek the unvarnished truth in the countryside, focused on London as the outlet for their work. A significant majority of them lived there, including, of course, John Constable. Constable has now become such a significant figure that we single him out from the rest. But at the time he was just one of a whole army of artists – like John Linnell, William Henry Hunt, William Mulready, Cornelius Varley – dedicated to setting down the 'truth' of local scenery. Like Constable, these artists saw moral and patriotic dimensions in such naturalism. They were reminding the nation of the heart of England. Often there was an intentional symbolism in their subjects. They tended to favour the representation of river scenes where trade and commerce could be seen. For it was a sign of the health of Britain that the economic system could be seen to be fuelled by the wealth of the countryside, the traditional site of the true and natural way of life.

I have already mentioned that it was in the context of the Napoleonic wars that talk of a 'British School' first arose. However, at this time attention was focused largely on history painting. The artistic establishment wanted to show that they had better history painters than the French. Incredibly, they really do seem to have believed that such jaded followers of Reynolds as Westall and Northcote were a match for David and his followers in Paris. Where this linked with landscape painting was in the belief that such history painting was better than the French because it was more natural. David – the hated regicide – had an artificial style of history painting, they argued, that fitted his inhumanity in supporting the French Revolution and signing the death warrant of the king of France. Landscape painting may not have been allowed into the pantheon of the greatest art. But it could still show its Britishness by being natural, by emphasising itself as the product of a country whose laws and institutions were based on those of nature, rather than on artificial constructs like those of the French.

In this climate of opinion there were genuine changes of practice amongst landscape painters. There was a greater emphasis, above all, on a sense of vividness and sensation. One of the signs of this is the significant increase in the practice of 'plein-air' oil painting, of making studies directly before nature. Plein-air painting is a very important issue. From the late eighteenth century to the early twentieth century it became the keymark of 'progressive' art, the sign of painting dealing directly with the truthfulness of things, with nature unsullied by law and convention. Only with the advent of Cubism did it seriously lose its status as the talisman of pictorial truth. We know Constable to have been an important practitioner of it, and see it as being the critical factor later on in the success of the French Impressionists. Because it is so intimately tied up with direct observation, it might seem to be a celebration of the local

and specific. So it is as well to recall that it was nothing of the sort in the first instance. In fact the practice began in Rome, in the seventeenth century. Claude himself is reported to have used it, as a means of gaining the experience to enhance the transcendent atmospherics of the background distances in his works. As anyone who has studied plein-air painting knows, it bears no necessary relation to topographical accuracy. It was practised in the first place to sharpen awareness of tone, atmosphere and colour. In the eighteenth century plein-air paintings were made by landscape painters from all over Europe who went to Rome, such as Valenciennes from France and Dillis from Germany. Wilson was probably the British exponent who imported the practice into England. But the one who is now known best for it of this generation is Thomas Jones. Jones is a fascinating figure, who has been rescued from relative obscurity this century. After studying with Wilson he went to Rome between 1776 and 1783. While there he made some remarkable landscapes studies. Then he came home and lived the life of a country gentleman. His wonderful plein-air work was not known until the 1950s, when it was discovered in a family attic. Hence this artist, hailed in recent years as an innovator of naturalism, was virtually unknown to his contemporaries.

However, while the personal example of Jones may not have counted for much in his own day, his work is symptomatic of the new attitude towards plein-air painting. For it shows a new concern to give authority to the directly experienced visual record, to gain a new closeness to nature. As such it can be seen as an important expression of that yearning for natural truth that marked the whole Romantic movement. It is significant, I think, that it parallels developments in the nature poetry of the day. In the 1790s Wordsworth and Coleridge attempted to develop new and more vivid experiences of nature, going for long walks in the countryside, notebook in hand, describing sensations as directly as possible before the motif. Coleridge even likened this practice to that of a painter making sketches.[5]

Plein-air painting was a common form of study in the early nineteenth century. But Constable's use of the genre was in a class of its own. No other landscape painter of the period is known to have practised it to the extent that he did. Indeed, his method seems to have involved a remarkable redundancy. For, like other landscape painters of the period, he did not use plein-air as a way of making completed pictures for exhibition and sale (there are only two instances where he appears to have done this). Some of his plein-air studies were used as material for finished pictures. Most of them weren't. Indeed a large number of them were of kinds of scenery and natural effects that he never used in his finished works at all. But it is not the sheer numbers even that are most significant. It is the level of engagement and enquiry that they represent. Constable was a painter full of uncertainty: uncertainty, I should add, of the right kind, for it led to the relentless and persisting pursuit of a problem. In this way he resembles Cézanne – as he does in his obsession with scenes that have personal associations for him. What gives Constable's sketches such excitement is the sense that they are created for themselves, rather than as preparation for a 'finished' picture already planned. They suggest a direct and intense engagement with the phenomena of nature.

It is also worth pointing out that this side of Constable was hardly known to his contemporaries at all. It was only after his daughter Isobel bequeathed the contents of his studio to the nation in the later nineteenth century that they came to be known beyond a small circle. Like Thomas Jones, Constable the plein-air painter was all but invisible in his own lifetime.

Constable the exhibition painter, too, was largely overlooked until the last part of his life. I shall return to this last part when considering the development of landscape painting after the Napoleonic wars. For the time being I want to continue by considering the kind of public landscape that was admired around 1800. Such pictures were not the portrayal of local scenery, the 'tame delineation of a given spot' as Fuseli described it, but the kind of imaginative landscape painting that combined nature with some important human or spiritual event: in a word, historical landscape. The leading exponent of this was J. M. W. Turner. Nowadays Turner and Constable are seen as the two great rival geniuses of British landscape. They seem to complement each other in their exploration of natural effect, Constable intensively studying a local, deeply personalised scenery, Turner ranging through every variety of landscape available to him, from the most dramatic to the most quiet. But we

should remember that, at the time, Turner was the celebrity and Constable hardly known at all. Turner had had a meteoric rise to prominence in the 1790s. In 1802, when he was only twenty-seven, he was made a full academician. Constable had to wait for that honour until 1829, when he was fifty-three. Turner's technical virtuosity – evident already in the early topographical water-colours he exhibited in the Royal Academy as a teenager – was important in gaining him recognition. But it was equally important that he took historical landscape painting seriously, and breathed new life into it. Typically Turner attempted all kinds of historical landscape – from severe classical pastiches to celebrations of modern life. But above all he was able to infuse historical landscape with the new Romantic sense of the importance of nature in the affairs of man. In particular he was completely up to date in seeing this relationship as a puzzling and mysterious one. Ideologically he was a pessimist, who saw man as isolated in an indifferent universe. His favourite contemporary poet was Byron, and he shared much of his hero's sense of irony. Turner had ambitions as a poet himself and worked for decades on a long epic poem that sought to express this view. Its title was *Fallacies of Hope*. Yet while Turner's view of human destiny was pessimistic, he clearly found its contemplation exhilarating. He was a true member of his generation in seeking sublime effect in disaster. This can be seen in such portrayals of tragedy as *The Shipwreck* (1805), in which he shows hapless survivors struggling in an awe-inspiring storm. Such works inspired enthusiasm amongst his contemporaries for their gripping subject matter. But they were also innovative pictorially, both from the point of view of their compositions and in the ways that they showed a more experimental way of handling paint and colour. For Turner was too great an artist not to understand the necessary interrelation between theme and treatment. He explored the world of vision as he explored the fate of man. He forged new ways of using paint to record emotive experience. Interestingly, he only practised plein-air painting on rare occasions. He was working with a more internalised form of experimentation in which memory and feeling were as important as direct observation. If Constable is the father of British naturalism, then Turner must be seen as the progenitor of the psychological landscape. His challenging vision has been seen far less often than that of Constable as the basis of a British landscape tradition. Yet it has been equally important in the landscape practice that has developed in this country.

In considering the development of sublime and historical landscape on the one hand, and of naturalism on the other, I have left out one other dimension of the art of the period that has been widely admired in our own century. This is the use of landscape to convey visionary experience that emerged in the work of Blake, and that of Samuel Palmer and his associates. This interest can be seen to grow out of the Romantic obsession with perceiving the divine in nature. While a small and isolated phenomenon in the visual arts in England, it has interesting parallels with a similar development in Germany, particularly in the works of the landscape painter Caspar David Friedrich. So close is some of their work that it has been asked if there can be a connection. Perhaps there is, but more important is the fact that they both drew inspiration from a visionary Protestant tradition that leads back to such mystics as the Bohemian Jacob Boehme. What is striking is that this type of visionary sentiment should now be expressed in pictures, whereas traditionally it had only existed in verbal form. It is certainly striking that inspiration for all these artists was originally poetic and religious. In the case of Blake – a major poet – this is self-evident. It is striking that he only attempted landscape at the end of his life when he already had a rich experience of describing natural effects in words. And when he did, it was in terms of engravings, where the image is presented in bold synoptic form, like a verbal metaphor. His follower Samuel Palmer continued this verbal interest. But he tried as well to 'see' his image, moving with associates to the village of Shoreham in Kent where they wore long flowing robes, called themselves 'The Ancients' and tried to get back to the primitive splendour of the pastoral world of the Bible. Perhaps because of being inspired by words, their images are striking for the boldness and richness – and bear very little reference to the observed world. They are more like stained-glass windows than naturalistic sketches. Indeed Palmer himself was a strong opponent of naturalism – which he saw as the equivalent of materialism.

In style Palmer's work could not have been further from Constable's. Yet he shared Constable's love of tradition and was equally upset by the sense that the rural way of life was being undermined by encroachments from the city. In his case this feeling led to the destruction of his confidence in his own visionary powers. In later life he produced wistful water-colours that lacked the intensity of his earlier work. Others of his group similarly softened their manner in line with the new sentimental form of the rural idyll. John Linnell was the most successful of these. His lyrical scenes of rural bliss – tinged with wistfulness – set the tone for a significant section of Victorian landscape painting.

While Palmer and the Ancients pursued a poetic and essentially intimate form of visionary art, spirituality also had its place in large-scale public paintings. Turner himself pursued the visionary side of art – moving increasingly towards the exploration of transcendent atmospheric effect in exhibited works, to the puzzlement of most of his contemporaries. He also increased the private side of his practice. For while he continued to exhibit up to a year before his death in 1851, he devoted a significant amount of his energies to the creation of canvases that were never exhibited, and perhaps were never intended to be. Unlike his exhibited works, these pictures rarely contain much narrative; though they are almost invariably tied to the representation of some natural effect. They are full of the glory of the primal power of light and colour, the expression of natural forces through the simulacra of paint. Discovered in his studio after his death, these pictures have never been accounted for satisfactorily in terms of the conventions of the practice of painting of his day. Yet whatever his intentions in creating them, they remain powerful demonstrations of the fact that painting engages the private world of the artist before it reaches the public.

While Turner's sublime vision developed an increasingly private dimension, there were other artists who explored the spiritual landscape on a popular level. The most successful of these was the Northumbrian painter John Martin. Significantly these popular landscapes remained within the purview of conventional religion. In them – as in the Old Testament – God is on the side of the righteous. They appealed to the popular imagination, and it is no surprise to see that they make full use of those theatrical devices that had been introduced by the scene painters – including huge variations of scale. Nor was there anything hypocritical about this. John Martin was devoutly religious. He spent the last years of his life completing a huge trilogy on the Last Judgement expressed in terms of sublime landscape. There was a touch of the primitive in Martin's vision, and it was probably this that gave him such an unerring feel for popular taste in these matters. It also gave his work a freshness, which is one of the reasons why his art can still excite today.

Turner, Palmer and Martin represent in their different ways the more internalised and dramatic sides of the practice of landscape painting at the time. Their affinities with the Romantic literature of the period are evident. Yet their emphasis on the subjective, the mysterious, the frightening meant that they did not form the basis of an 'English landscape tradition'. It was only in the mid twentieth century, with a reawakening of interest in Romantic subjectivity, that they began to become significant from this point of view. In the nineteenth century it was the image of tranquil rural life that dominated in contemporary landscape painting.

It was in the period following the Napoleonic wars that naturalism came to be seen as the normative English form of art. A critical moment in this process was the exhibition of Hogarth's work at the British Institution in 1814, when it became possible to appreciate his qualities as a painter as well as an engraver. But the taste for nature had already been exploited by genre painters, in particular David Wilkie. Landscape painting at this time, indeed, was seen as the adjunct and handmaid of genre, providing the stage, so to speak, on which the idyllic life of the British rustic could be acted out. There were numerous publications that reinforced this growing shift, but the one that sealed it was Alan Cunningham's *Lives of the Most Eminent British Artists* of 1830–32. Cunningham was a friend and support of Wilkie and a great supporter of the notion that British art was essentially naturalistic, on account of its necessary relationship with British empiricism and the Protestant tradition.

The emergence of the argument in the post-Napoleonic period is revealing. For on the one hand the recent victories in Europe had given the British the comforting sense of being top nation, and of being more confident about their culture. But it also reflected an anxiety. For there was the fear that all was to be given away by sullying the great British Protestant tradition with cultural inroads. Cunningham wrote at the moment when the first wave of this fear existed. For in 1829 the Catholics had been allowed emancipation. And there was talk of a concomitant political crisis – that of the Reform Bill that would allow in 1832 the new urban populations to have more of a voice in Parliament. The image of the British naturalist tradition was forged in a climate where a vested interest was seeking cultural arguments to protect itself against inroads into its power.

It is worth recording that Constable was completely at one with those conservatives who invoked the English spirit in culture as an argument against change. Coming from a minor landowning family he was an absolute supporter of the regime – however corrupt – that gave power to the rural aristocrats. He was, as well, a devout member of the established church. His closest friend, John Fisher, was an Anglican archdeacon. His letters in the 1820s are full of pessimistic statements about the present state of the country, linked in with patriotic outbursts. In 1821, he regretted never having been to Italy to see 'the living scenes that inspired the landscapes of . . . Claude. But I was born to paint a happier land, my own dear old England; and when I cease to love her, may I, as Wordsworth says, "never more hear her green leaves rustle, and her torrents roar"'.

And when, in the 1830s, he sought to have his work commemorated in a series of mezzotints, he entitled it 'The English Landscape'. It was this public, patriotic side of Constable's art that was known to his contemporaries, and which was first celebrated in a national collection. After his death his friends presented *The Cornfield* to the National Gallery, a picture that conjures up an image of rural peace and tranquillity – together with the sentimentality of childhood. It is significant that Constable's first (and greatest) biographer, C. R. Leslie, was a painter of sentimental genre scenes. For it was such artists who developed the side of Constable's work that evoked the rural idyll. While there were no major artists who could have been said to have taken up the challenge of Constable's art in the Victorian period, he did inspire a whole population of minor but highly popular depicters of English rural life and scenery, reaching from William Collings and Thomas Webster in the 1840s to Vicat Cole and Benjamin Williams Leader at the turn of the century.

Nor has this emulation ever ceased. There can hardly be an art society in the country that does not exhibit works that show the imprint of Constable to this day.

The tragedy for Constable was that he began his career celebrating a vigorous and thriving way of life – that of the rural bourgeoisie – and ended it by becoming the model for urban sentimentalisations about the countryside. It was for this reason that he appealed so little to those progressive artists in the mid nineteenth century who were still trying to work with a notion of pictorial authenticity. The year in which Leslie's *Life of Constable* was published, 1843, was also the year in which the first volume of a work by a remarkable new critic appeared. Ruskin's *Modern Painters* became the talisman for the young Pre-Raphaelite painters. They took to heart his dictum that the aspiring artist should go to nature 'selecting nothing, rejecting nothing'. Ruskin's own vision of nature was heroic and universal. He had little time for Constable, who he thought had viewed nature in too narrow and blinkered a fashion. His hero was Turner, battling with the elements, representing nature in all her moods. He insisted on detailed study because he thought that was the way to penetrate through to the heart of the natural world. This intensive exploration was for him a spiritual as well as an intellectual experience. For he believed that nature, if looked at properly, gave evidence of the power and benevolence of the deity.

On the face of it, it must seem curious that Ruskin's influence should have been more on the side of stimulating meticulous painting, than on the side of promoting heroic, panoramic visions of nature. But the problem was that his pantheism was out of date. It came from an earlier generation of Romantics. In mid-Victorian England it was very hard to look at nature and see evidence of the power of the deity. For the increasingly urban society nature had become a tame affair. There was more fear of social disintegration and revolution than there was of the force of an avalanche or a storm at sea. There was even a growing doubt that the divine hand could be seen at all in nature – particularly after the publication of Darwin's *Origin of Species* in 1859. This was the milieu the Pre-Raphaelites lived in. Their principal inspiration was the past, the medieval world where women were women and men were men, and the earth glittered with the primal colours of paradise. Encouraged by Ruskin, they studied nature in detail. They innovated the practice of completely painting their landscapes out of doors, before the motif. But try as they might, they could not find what they were looking for. They ransacked the countryside, turned over every pebble and blade of grass. But still they could not find the pot of gold that Ruskin had promised them. The intensiveness in their art is the intensiveness of longing. They were better off on the whole when they devoted themselves to evoking the never-never land of yesteryear. They knew then that they were dreaming.

Heroic landscape was no longer possible for artists living in mid-Victorian Britain – or indeed, in most of the urbanised western world. Only in America, where a frontier society was forging west through stupendous scenery and treacherous terrain, could naturalistic painters like Frederick Church still perceive nature as heroic during this period.

European culture at this time was more concerned with urban problems. In the literature of the period one finds emerging a new kind of scene painting, that of the urban or industrial landscape. It has often been remarked that British painters of the later nineteenth century are surprisingly loath to engage in the contemplation of such environments. There was, it is true, a kind of jolly representation of modern life in the mid-Victorian world – pioneered by the panoramic surveys of William Powell Frith in such works as *The Railway Station*. There were, too, occasional spillages from this genre into the survey scenes of life in the industrial north. Most famous of these nowadays (though little regarded in its own time) is Eyre Crowe's *Wigan Girls at Lunchtime*, now in Manchester City Art Gallery. Yet these swallows hardly made a summer. There is a huge contrast here with the engagement with urbanism that is at the heart of the Impressionist movement which was gathering strength in France at the same time.

One can, of course, mount all sorts of speculations as to why this should be so. In contrast to France, the British perception of urbanism at this time was largely negative. We had no emperor taking our capital by the scruff of the neck and sprucing it into a swanky display of pleasure and ceremony. In contrast to Paris – as it was remodelled by Napoleon III after 1851 – London was mean and dirty. It showed the modern capitalist economy in the raw. Novelists like Dickens could write about it with censure. Illustrators could do it too, as the Frenchman Doré did in his searing expose of the city's low life, *London*, in 1872. But painters of pictures were expected to obey different principles in those days; to celebrate the beautiful or the sublime – not perpetuate the sordid.

This situation can be seen reflected in the work of the one artist who might have become the bastion of a modern school of urban landscape in London. The American James Abbot McNeil Whistler came to settle in London around 1860 after having studied in Paris. He was fully aware of the current realist movement in France and was to keep in touch with later developments. He came to know the Impressionist circle well, and was particularly close to that arch-urbanist Degas. When Whistler first came to London he set about celebrating the urban world. Like so many of the French writers of the day (such as Gautier) he admired the 'spleen' of the modern monster metropolis. He travelled to the grimier quarters of the Thames and made records in etchings and paintings of the low life of the river. In such works he was looking firmly at the modern world, and celebrating its heroic nature in true Baudelairean fashion. But the longer Whistler stayed in England, the more he moved away from this. He fell under the spell of the Pre-Raphaelites – Rossetti in particular – and began to paint wan, ethereal women. He rejected realism, and espoused instead aestheticism. Nature ceased to be a bible. It became instead his dictionary, out of which he would select the effect he wanted. In his later work he delighted still in painting poor, and even industrial scenes. But now he has imposed on these a veil of beauty of his own imagining. His painting of *Battersea Bridge* in the Tate Gallery bears this out. It is of a poor part of London. There are warehouses in the distance. But we see it as a remake of an elegant Japanese print. The main message here is the right of the artist to impose his personality on nature as he wills.

Just as there was little in the way of realistic portrayal of the urban landscape at this time, so representations of the countryside continued to ignore the increasing problems of rural society. There is virtually nothing in the landscape painting of the period to match the pessimism expressed by new writers on life in the countryside like Richard Jefferies and Thomas Hardy. Those novelists saw old rural communities being broken on the wheel of modern urbanism. But such painters as went into the countryside at that time came back with stories of a tough, healthy people, the salt of the earth, and the reassurance that out there in the rural community the good old heart of England was still beating firm and strong. The late Victorian period was the time when artists' colonies began to be established in remote and primitive parts of the country. The most famous of these was the community at Newlyn in Cornwall, established by Stanhope Forbes in 1885. Like so many painters in England at that time, the Newlyn painters were heavily influenced by French realism. But they used the modern continental style to tell folk tales of good old British stalwarts.

Whistler's position as the chief representative of the avant-garde undoubtedly had a strong effect on the way progressive art was perceived in Britain at the time. Unfortunately it also seems to have polarised some artists back into the adoption of a defensive Britishness. The 'alternative' to Whistlerian modernism in the last decades of the nineteenth century was a form of Impressionism that seemed as keen to revive a 'British tradition' as it was to engage contemporary developments in France. This can be seen in particular in the New English Art Club, established in 1886 as a breakaway group from the Royal Academy. The disconcerting words 'new' and 'art' in their title (suggestive of suspect continental ways) are counterbalanced by the reassuringly national words 'English' and 'club'. The group rapidly became associated with a British version of Impressionism – particularly in the work of Sickert and Wilson Steer. But while this work was originally innovative it became more and more tied up with a re-perception of the work of Constable. It is typical of this move that the leading figures in this English club came to oppose anything that smacked of Whistlerism. This included rejecting the work of the 'Glasgow Boys' – an exciting group of progressive Scottish artists who had originally been their allies. It is striking how many artists in Scotland began to explore paths that deviated from anglocentric norms at this time and came far closer to developments on the Continent. Doubtless the revival of a sense of Celtic culture – a reaction in itself to the centralised promotion of Englishness – played its part. The new focus on international – as opposed to English – art, also liberated artists in the older generation. One notable example of this is the later work of William MacTaggart, one of the most original landscape painters working in the British Isles around 1900. MacTaggart paintings of this period have an affinity with the late plays of Ibsen in their mixture of realistic observation with a mystical sense of the forces of nature.

The New English Art Club did not favour such experimentation. Under the guidance of their principal mentor, Philip Wilson Steer, they promoted a dialogue with earlier forms of English naturalism, in particular the works of Constable. Because they were seeing Constable through the eyes of the Impressionists, they emphasised his sketch-like nature, supporting the preference for his studies to his finished oils. It is also symptomatic of this change that Turner's 'unfinished' works began to attract new attention. It was in the Edwardian period that they were put on show first at the National Gallery and then at the Tate.

The continued demand for this impressionistic version of the English tradition is borne out by the fact that, to this day, the New English Art Club flourishes and promotes work distinctly in the tradition of its early members.

I have said that there was little urban or industrial landscape in Britain at the time. But there was a notable exception in the work of Sickert. Sickert eventually broke away both from Whistler and from the New English Art Club. Often abroad, he stormed in and out of English artistic life in the early twentieth century like a whirlwind. His own depictions of music halls and the seedier aspects of city life provided a dimension to British urban art that had hitherto been missing. Through his leading position in the setting up of the Camden Town group he set up a tradition of realistic representation of urban disquiet that has persisted up to the present. His presence can be felt lurking behind much of the work of the Euston Road group, and there is still some kind of dialogue in play between his pictures and those of Frank Auerbach and Lucien Freud.

The Sickertian tendency (tradition would be too strong a word for it) involved a turning away from the re-interpretation of the British landscape tradition as promoted by the New English Art Club. This resurrected practice was also challenged by more progressive forms of modernism, in particular the abstracting 'Post-Impressionist' dimensions perceived and promoted by Roger Fry in the years before the First World War. While centrally dependent on the example of Cézanne, it also supported a new kind of primitivism. This made it possible for artists like Augustus John and J. D. Innes to look anew at British rural life and scenery and to celebrate a more vibrant and primal image – the world of gypsies and wild Wales. Rather sadly, much of the energy of this youthful upsurge became dissipated. In the case of John he seems to have been overtaken rapidly by the romanticised image of his own bohemianism.

The dissipation of this radical, primitivising approach to landscape can be associated with the outbreak of the First World War. This was true in a literal sense – for the careers of many artists were interrupted or destroyed through their involvement in the war. But there was also the effect it had in leading to the questioning of some of the assumptions in landscape painting. In the last great European conflict, the Napoleonic wars, landscape had been used both in England and elsewhere to promote patriotism. The looming northern forests of Caspar David Friedrich and the thriving Thames-side scenes of Turner had been part of the war effort in their respective countries. But the landscapes of the First World War were quite different. For here, along the Western Front, was a countryside being shattered by man. Nature was war's victim, alongside the common soldier. It did not symbolise resistance to the enemy. It was a plea against war of any kind. Its commentary was aesthetic as well as political. The disfigured landscape frequently evoked 'abstract' forms of Cubism, suggesting to some that modernism destroyed as it transformed. Some modernists prior to the First World War – such as the Futurists in Italy, the Vorticists in England and the Expressionists in Germany – had looked to war as a kind of bloodletting that would sweep away the old order and usher in the modern age. Now, in the heat of conflict, it seemed that the creatures of this brave new world were nothing but hideous monsters. But fire could be fought with fire: for modernism had given to landscape a new power that enabled it to move beyond 'mere' representation to engage in deeper psychological issues. As with English war poetry (for example that of Wilfred Owen) the armoury of modernism could be used to re-equip a traditional mode. Amongst the many British landscape painters who depicted the tragedy using a fusion of modernised form and traditionist sentiment Paul Nash was perhaps the most successful. His *We are Making a New World*, showing a shattered copse, expresses the situation with characteristic irony. He wrote when at the front: 'One can't think which is the more absurd, the War or Nature; the former has become a habit so confirmed, inevitable, it has the grip on the world just as surely as spring or summer.'[6]

Yet in the end war lost its hold on the cycle of nature. Afterwards, the dialogue between modernity and tradition took on a different pattern, invoking harmony and order. In a society shattered by the trauma of conflict this is hardly surprising. In the visual arts it was a time for moderation, when many erstwhile Vorticists abandoned their sharp geometry for more tactile forms. This is perhaps most notable in the work of David Bomberg, who began the long and isolated progress towards the painterly expressionism of his last years. 'Craft' became an issue once again. It was the age of Eric Gill, David Jones and the revival of wood engraving. There was also a new dimension to the propagandist exploitation of the rural idyll. The therapy and solace of the countryside was now being promoted for the masses. Day-trippers and hikers came to join the weekend cottagers. Visual images of a pleasant, friendly rural England became the commonplace of posters, biscuit tins and place mats as well as fine art paintings.

These democratic intrusions into the actual and imagined countryside stimulated an increasing gap between sophisticated and vulgar responses to the countryside. The Edwardian era was perhaps the last time when there remained some remote parts of the British Isles that could still be seen as virgin territory by the urban excursionist. Now there was only one way to avoid the crowd. And that was to go inwards. Nothing characterises the sophisticated appreciation of the British landscape in the twentieth century more than the sense of privacy, even secrecy. Spurred on by the assertions of psychology – that modern substitute for the spiritual – the countryside became internalised, mysterious and

symbolic. In the visual arts the conventions of modernism could be used to stimulate a new game of allusiveness. It is perhaps significant that this was the time when plein-air painting began to lose its appeal for the avant-garde artist. That kind of thing is left to local art societies and amateurs now. The modern painter relates to nature in more complex and enigmatic ways.

One consequence of the emergence of the psychological landscape was that it led to the creation of a new genealogy for the British tradition. The more intimate side of Romanticism now became the model. New prominence was given the sketches of Constable and the puzzling unexhibited pictures of Turner's later years. One of the most significant discoveries in the 1920s was the early work of Samuel Palmer. Most of this had lain unseen in the hands of his family. Indeed, a shocking amount of it had actually been destroyed by his son, who feared it might damage the reputation he was hoping to revive for his father's later conventional Victorian water-colours. Now the Shoreham period pictures, with their exciting combination of primitivism and intimacy, became admired. A whole generation of students from Goldsmiths' College in London appear to have been nurtured on this rich lore – the most significant being Graham Sutherland.

The psychological landscape also affected the valuation of the primitive. Here there was an easy rapprochement, for the Romantics themselves had been the initiators of the admiration of the primitive by western man. Now the primitive could be seen in a more universalist light, embracing world culture and extracting from each society those features that seemed to reinforce the idea of an underlying spirituality in artistic expression. It also led to the discovery by avant-garde artists of traditional 'naive' painters at work in Britain – such as the retired Cornish fisherman Alfred Wallis, who was taken up by Ben Nicholson, Christopher Wood and other members of the St Ives community. Some painters managed to negotiate the terrain between modernism and primitivism with great skill. In their very different ways both Stanley Spencer and L. S. Lowry profited from the opportunities on offer. Both exaggerated the extent of their proletarian origins to gain the licence to describe their local scenery with a regional accent. Lowry managed to create one of the few enduring representations of the northern industrial landscape – albeit in a somewhat sentimentalised and stereotyped manner. Spencer explored a richer and more challenging vision of the scenery of his native Cookham in the Thames Valley. With their remarkable adaptation of Pre-Raphaelite intensity and modernist perspective, their yoking of contemporary psychosexuality to conventional religion, his paintings represent one of the high points of British twentieth-century landscape painting. All the more remarkable that so many of them were painted under pressure, and for financial reasons.

The 1930s are widely seen as a time when British art moved once again towards the mainstream of modern art. The activities of the 7+5 society (which had Ben Nicholson and Barbara Hepworth amongst its members) and the Unit One group showed a resolute engagement with forms of abstraction and, a little later, with Surrealism. Yet it is also striking to see that so much of this engagement was undertaken in terms of landscape and the forms of nature. Henry Moore and Barbara Hepworth may have admired the a priori geometries of the Russian constructivist Naum Gabo and the Dutch de Stijl painter Piet Mondrian. But in their own work abstraction was always more empirical, closer to the experience of nature. I think it is fair to say that these artists felt themselves as having to make some kind of rapprochement between a local practice and the radical innovations of continental art. This is certainly the attitude expressed by their colleague Paul Nash in his article 'Being British and Going Modern'. There was as well, perhaps, a sense of Britain having a positive role to play as a mediator between the extremities of revolution and reaction. The 1930s, after all, were witnessing a gradual political polarisation on the Continent, with the Soviet Union representing one extreme and the Fascist regimes of Germany, Italy and Spain the other. Many of the continental abstract artists who arrived in Britain at this time did so as political refugees. Such experiences nurtured the growth of that fortress mentality that favoured so much the revival of British Romanticism in the late 1930s and during the period of the Second World War.

This attitude can be revealed most clearly in the British response to Surrealism. Surrealism was on the one hand a disturbingly radical movement. Emphasising the subconscious and the irrational, it drew on recent psychological theories and promoted anarchic behaviour. On the other hand it could also be seen as a protest against the over-regimentation of modernist formalism. In the visual arts it favoured representation and allusion and openly drew connections with Romanticism. The Surrealist movement was slow to arrive in Britain. It only really established itself in 1936, twelve years after it had been launched in Paris. This was the year in which an International Surrealist Exhibition was held in London. But if the movement came to Britain late, when it arrived it was seen more as a meeting than a conquest. Vigorously supported by the critic Herbert Read, then the leading apologist for modern art in Britain, the exhibition encompassed a large number of leading indigenous avant-garde artists, including Henry Moore and Paul Nash. It seems as though the British had been Surrealists all along without knowing it.

According to Herbert Read himself, the artists of this country were 'naturally' Surrealist. The whole tradition of British fantasy – leading back to the Romantics and encompassing nonsense poets like Edward Lear and Lewis Carroll – proclaimed this. It seemed as though the individualism and anarchy of Surrealism were tailor-made for the local temperament. There may be something in this – to judge by the extent that Surrealism has remained an active element in British popular and commercial culture ever since (witness the success of the Goon Show, The Beatles and Monty Python). Be that as it may, this 'recognition' had the advantage of enabling artists to engage with Surrealism without having to capitulate to it. On the whole those British artists who accepted continental Surrealism wholesale achieved little of distinction; whereas those – like Nash and Moore – who melded it with their existing practice, found the experience to be an enriching one.

It has already been mentioned that the response to Surrealism in Britain was mediated partly through the revival of interest in Romanticism. But it is equally true to say that the revival of interest in Romanticism itself was shaped to some extent by developments in both Surrealism and other areas of modernist art. It is no accident that the visual work of Blake underwent a reassessment through the activities of the Bloomsbury circle, or that the early and most radical work of Samuel

Palmer was 'rediscovered' and put on show first in the 1920s. Similarly, the more unfinished work of Turner and the sketches of Constable stimulated a new interest at this time. Indeed, it was only through the discernment of critics and museum curators with a taste for modern art that the most extreme of Turner's late canvases were recognised to be pictures and were put on show at the National Gallery and the Tate. Such magnificent late pictures by Turner as *Yacht Approaching the Coast* were only put on show at the Tate Gallery in the 1930s. It was in this climate that landscape painters like Graham Sutherland and Ivon Hitchens first came to produce their particular fusion of modernism and Romanticism in their works.

The use of modernism to rediscover Romanticism was, not surprisingly, seen as a retrogressive step by many continental observers. Nikolaus Pevsner, one of the emigrés to this country in the 1930s, certainly felt that this marked the British contribution and made them incapable of leadership in modern art: 'If England seems so far incapable of leadership in twentieth-century painting, the extreme contrast between the spirit of the age and English qualities is responsible. Art in her leaders is violent today; it breaks up more than it yet reassembles. England dislikes violence and believes in evolution'.[7]

Yet the re-engagement with landscape that had been opened up by Surrealism had led in fact to remarkable innovations. One of the most striking of these was the extension of landscape art into a predominantly figurative art form – that of sculpture. It might seem strange to move at this point from a discussion of painting to that of sculpture. Yet I believe it is utterly appropriate – indeed important – to do so. The one thing that has kept the practice of landscape alive in this country has been its ability to suggest new ideas and new directions. When modern sculpture moved away from figurative representation under the impact of Cubism, it was already moving towards areas closer to painting. Now the Surrealist doctrine of chance meetings allowed a whole new area of imagery to be set in motion in the shapes and spaces of three-dimensional form.

Henry Moore is a key figure in this development. As an artist attracted to Surrealism, psychology and the ability to use the figure more imaginatively, he brought landscape elements directly into his own sculptures. We can see this in his forms of the 1930s, in his bringing together of the found object in nature with that of the abstract sculpture. Moore has figures in landscape and landscape in figures.

Moore's position was shared by other sculptors of his generation – notably Barbara Hepworth. More importantly he opened up a dialogue that has continued ever since. It has often been remarked how strong sculpture has been in this country since the time of Hepworth and Moore. Perhaps one reason for this has been the continued space it has provided for the dialogue between 'modern' abstraction and traditional perception of nature. It is possible to trace this influence through successive permutations. The metal constructions of Anthony Caro replace Moore's 'natural' materials and sculptural forms with those of modern industrial processes. Yet the open-spaced nature of his forms maintains a dialogue with landscape. Even those of his followers who moved towards the use of more modern and synthetic materials – such as Phillip King – retained this spatial engagement. Interestingly, British landscape sculpture met up in the 1960s with the landscape tradition of the United States. Robert Smithson, in particular, was forging a link between the American sublime and new forms of earth sculpture. This linkage formed a seemingly natural context for the land-art forms innovated by Richard Long and Hamish Fulton at this time. To a large extent such artists have seen themselves as continuing and developing practices established in the Romantic era. Long, for example, has compared himself to Turner in his 'heroic' quest to experience the extremities of nature. Another intriguing affinity between this new art form and Romantic landscape can be found in the shared interest in language. This can be witnessed in particular in the work of the poet-sculptor Iain Hamilton Finlay. Long and Finlay have been around for some time, but the practice is by no means wearing thin. Its continued potency can be seen in the work of many younger artists, in particular in the elegant and enigmatic constructions of Andy Goldsworthy.

This is not to say that other avenues for landscape art have closed. If any lesson is to be learned from changes in artistic activity over the last two decades, it is that there is no straight lineal flow in the succession of styles and practices that come to prominence. They have always to be seen in relation to the rich undercurrent of alternatives that are kept alive in more secretive ways, which mercifully enable them to survive. In fact much of the tendency towards abstraction in Britain in the mid-century remained faithful to the sense of landscape. This is evident even in the work of such devotees of formal abstraction as Ben Nicholson. In the post-war period, that bailiwick of Ben Nicholson and Barbara Hepworth, the St Ives School, maintained an attachment to a strongly nature-based form of abstraction. The leading figure in this group – Peter Lanyon – continued to refer to himself as a landscape painter, and his pictures are rich with references to Cornish places. Throughout the years of Pop, Op, and Conceptualism, painters like Ivon Hitchens, John Piper and Cedric Morris kept working quietly, living largely in the depths of the country, supported by faithful followers. All of them brought a modern sensibility to landscape. They were painters of the twentieth century and did not turn their backs on the complexities of contemporary experience or artistic expression. But the world they looked at was not that of the modern city. And if they spoke to that world (as they did – while not always being appreciated by those who thought art should be about the celebration of modernity), then they were reminding it of the fact that there still is a nature active beyond society. They were a warning to an age obsessed with self-referential structures that man must take seriously that which he cannot control, as well as that which he has created. Nature scorned will take its revenge. Their magnificent maverick pictures have proved touchstones for many artists involved in reassessing the landscape tradition since the early 1980s. It is perhaps too early to say how this re-assessment will turn out altogether. Some of the artists enthusiastically hailed as the leaders of a landscape revival a few years ago are beginning to look rather thin. But there are others who have emerged as mature and impressive voices. Amongst these must be numbered Maurice Cockrill and William Tillyer.

It will, I hope, have become clear from this survey, that, like all important artistic phenomena, the practice of landscape art in this country over the last two centuries has been intimately connected with broader developments within our society. Internally, this can be seen in terms of an increasingly urbanised, secularised and multi-cultural society having to redefine its position in relation to the natural environment. Externally it has been related to the position of Britain in the world at large. Our growing, seemingly inexorable decline has led to our having to redefine our position in relation to our own cultural traditions. Perhaps this is why there has been so much emphasis on inwardness in late twentieth-century British landscape art. When external conditions worsen it is a natural tendency to move towards more private worlds.

Privacy is sometimes seen as a malaise of our society. For both extremes of the political spectrum it represents a debilitating fragmentation that undermines the strength of the corporate body. But it can also be the site of reflection and realisation. At times like this, when almost every ideology appears bankrupt, the inner world is likely to prove the individual's most fruitful resource.

In such circumstances, it is important that landscape painting can awaken in us not just a sense of intimacy, but also of variety. For there is not much virtue at the moment in insisting on conformity to some norm, or in hailing a single development as the route to salvation. Rather than do this, therefore, I would like to end by invoking a metaphor that casts the development of landscape art into a natural form: that of the tree. There are many branches that spring from a tree-trunk, and they point in different directions. At first the branches are clearly distinguishable from the trunk. But after a while, as the trunk gets thinner, and the spreading branches more numerous and diverse, it is impossible to say any more which is which. Perhaps, indeed, there no longer is a trunk, though every branch has its own connection to the one that supports it from below. I like to think of the landscape art of this country like that. There are many fruitful branches flourishing at the moment, and one does not have an obvious ascendancy over the others. Let us hope that this pattern remains, and that no one will try to pollard the rich and variegated foliage back to a single stem.

NOTES

1. Nikolaus Pevsner, *The Englishness of English Art*, p. 193.

2. Linda Colley, *Britons: Forging the Nation, 1707–1836*, Yale University Press, 1992.

3. W. Vaughan, 'The Englishness of British Art' in *Oxford Art Journal*, 1990, vol. 13 no. 2, pp. 11–23.

4. Edmund Burke, *A Philosophical Enquiry into our Ideas of the Sublime and Beautiful*, 1757.

5. See Richard Holmes, *Coleridge: Early Visions*, 1989, p. 161.

6. Paul Nash, *An Autobiography and Other Writings*, 1949, p. 187.

7. Pevsner, *op. cit*, pp. 193–4.

Nicholas Alfrey studied fine art at Edinburgh, then art history at the Courtauld Institute of Art. Since 1977 he has lectured in art history at the University of Nottingham. He worked on the exhibition *Turner en France* at the Centre Culturel du Marais in Paris in 1981, and co-edited (with Stephen Daniel) *Mapping the Landscape: essays in art and cartography* (1990).

Paul Barker writes on architecure and planning for various publications (including *Modern Painters* and the London *Evening Standard*). Books he has edited include *Arts in Society* and *The Other Britain*. He was a founder-director of Pennine Heritage. From 1968 to 1986 he was editor of *New Society*, and he continues to write and broadcast regularly on social issues. He has just been awarded a Leverhulme research fellowship to work on a new book, *Journey into England*.

Margaret Drabble is a novelist and critic, author of twelve novels and editor of the fifth edition of the *Oxford Companion to English Literature* (1985). She has also written on Wordsworth and Arnold Bennett. Her most recent novel is *The Gates of Ivory* (1991). She is currently working on a biography of Angus Wilson. She lives partly in London, partly in Somerset, and is married to the biographer Michael Holroyd.

Norbert Lynton, Emeritus Professor of the History of Art at the University of Sussex and author of *The Story of Modern Art* and other books on art and architecture, including *William Scott* (1990), *Victor Pasmore* (1992) and *Ben Nicholson* (1993), taught in art schools (Leeds College of Art, Chelsea School of Art and the Royal College of Art), was director of exhibitions for the Arts Council of Great Britain and wrote art criticism regularly for *Art International* and *The Guardian* and occasionally for many other papers and journals.

Richard Mabey is a writer with a special interest in natural history and landscape. His books include *The Common Ground*, *The Flowering of Britain*, *Gilbert White* (which won the 1986 Whitbread Biography of the Year Award) and *Home Country*, which he describes as a 'landscape autobiography'. He contributes regularly to *Modern Painters*, *The Times* and *The Independent*. He is a director of the arts and conservation charity Common Ground, and lives in the Chilterns, where he owns and looks after a 'community woodland'.

David Matthews is a composer whose works include four symphonies, six string quartets and numerous other orchestral, chamber and vocal pieces. He also writes frequently on contemporary music, and is the author of *Michael Tippett: An Introductory Study* (1980) and the 1991 Peter Fuller Memorial Lecture on music and painting, *Landscape into Sound* (1992).

Adam Nicolson was born in 1957. He is the author of several books on travel and the landscape, including *Long Walks*, *Landscape in Britain*, *Frontiers* (winner of the Somerset Maugham Prize) and *Wetland* (winner of the British Topography Prize).

Kathleen Raine is a critic, poet and writer on Blake, whose work has been translated into several languages. Among her books are: *Selected Works of Thomas Taylor the Platonist*; *Blake and Antiquity*; *William Blake* in the Thames and Hudson World of Art series; *The Human Face of God*, on Blake's Job engravings; *Yeats the Initiate*; *Defending Ancient Springs* and *Golgonooza, Blake's City of Imagination*. She is the founder of the Temenos Academy of Integral Studies. Her most recently published poetry is *Living with Mystery: Poems 1987–91*; she was awarded the Queen's Medal for Poetry in 1992.

William Vaughan is Professor of History of Art at Birkbeck College, University of London. He has published on British and German art of the early nineteenth century. Among his books are *William Blake* (1977), *Romantic Art* (1978) and *German Romantic Painting* (1980). He has also organised exhibitions, including one on *Caspar David Friedrich* at the Tate Gallery in 1972. He has recently completed a book on *The Image of the Artist*.

Colour plates

1 Richard Wilson *View near Wynnstay, the Seat of Sir Watkin Williams-Wynne* 1770–71

2 Thomas Gainsborough *Heneage Lloyd and his Sister* 1750s

3 Thomas Gainsborough *Rocky Landscape* c. 1783

4   John Constable *Sketch for 'The Leaping Horse'* 1824–25

5 John Constable *Dedham Vale* 1828

6 J. M. W. Turner *Crossing the Brook* c. 1815

7 J. M. W. Turner *Norham Castle, Sunrise* c. 1845

8 Samuel Palmer *The Magic Apple Tree c.* 1830

9 William Holman Hunt *Our English Coasts (Strayed Sheep)* 1852

10 Stanley Spencer *A View of the Thames from Cockmarsh Hill, Cookham* 1935

11 Graham Sutherland *Road and Hills in Setting Sun* 1938

12 Ben Nicholson *Landscape with River and Trees, Cumberland* 1926

13 Ben Nicholson *Painted relief* 1941

14 Paul Nash *Farewell* 1944

15 Ivon Hitchens *Terwick Mill No. 11, Early Autumn* 1945

16 David Bomberg *Exmoor, Devon* 1946

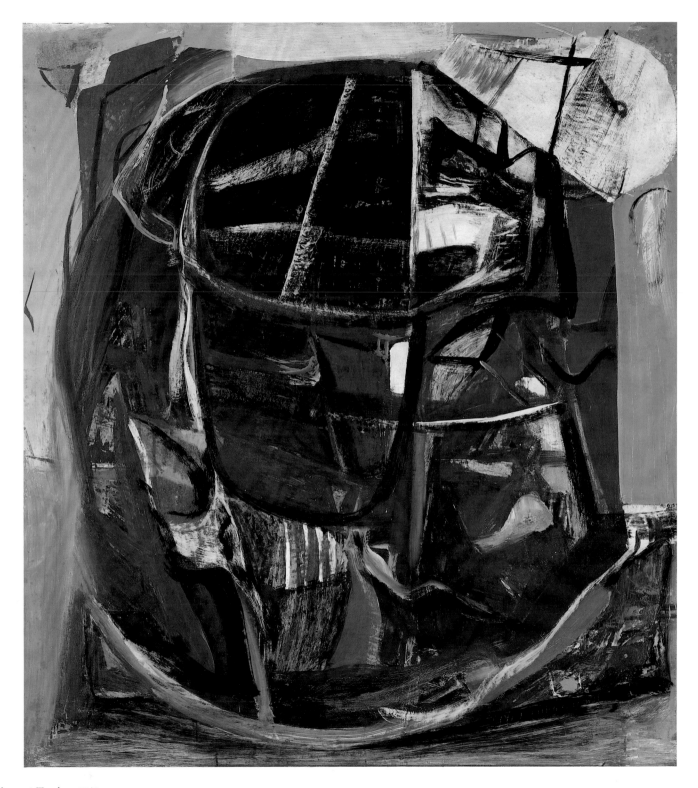

17 Peter Lanyon *Landscape at Trevalgan* 1951

18 Edward Burra *Near Whitby, Yorkshire* 1972

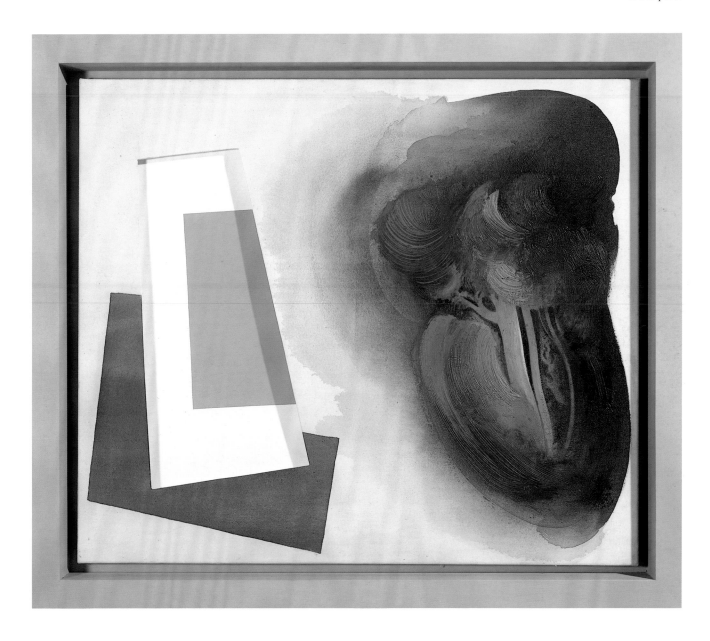

19 William Tillyer *Urra* 1992–93

20 Maurice Cockrill *Wheat Insemination* 1992

21 John Virtue *Landscape No. 178* 1992

22 Wendy Connelly *Snowdonia: Early Spring* 1993

1 Richard Wilson
*View near Wynnstay, the Seat of
Sir Watkin Williams-Wynne*
1770–71
oil on canvas, 71 × 96 in.
Yale Center for British Art,
Paul Mellon Collection

2 Thomas Gainsborough
Heneage Lloyd and his Sister
1750s
oil on canvas, 25 × 32 in.
Syndics of the Fitzwilliam Museum

3 Thomas Gainsborough
Rocky Landscape
c. 1783
oil on canvas, 45¾ × 56½ in.
National Gallery of Scotland

4 John Constable
Sketch for 'The Leaping Horse'
1824–25
oil on canvas, 51 × 74 in.
Board of Trustees of the Victoria
and Albert Museum

5 John Constable
Dedham Vale
1828
oil on canvas, 55½ × 48 in.
National Gallery of Scotland

6 J. M. W. Turner
Crossing the Brook
c. 1815
oil on canvas, 76 × 85 in.
Tate Gallery, London

7 J. M. W. Turner
Norham Castle, Sunrise
c. 1845
oil on canvas, 35¾ × 48 in.
Tate Gallery, London

8 Samuel Palmer
The Magic Apple Tree
c. 1830
pen, indian ink, water-colour and
gum arabic, 13½ × 10½ in.
Syndics of the Fitzwilliam Museum

9 William Holman Hunt
Our English Coasts (Strayed Sheep)
1852
oil on canvas, 17 × 23 in.
Tate Gallery, London

10 Stanley Spencer
*A View of the Thames from Cockmarsh
Hill, Cookham*
1935
oil on canvas, 27¼ × 35 in.
Waddington Galleries

11 Graham Sutherland
Road and Hills in Setting Sun
1938
oil on canvas, 24 × 20 in.
Private collection

12 Ben Nicholson
*Landscape with River and Trees,
Cumberland*
1926
oil on canvas, 24 × 34 in.
Bernard Jacobson Gallery

13 Ben Nicholson
Painted relief
1941
oil on board, 37½ × 35¾ in.
Bernard Jacobson Gallery

14 Paul Nash
Farewell
1944
oil on canvas, 20 × 24 in.
Bernard Jacobson Gallery

15 Ivon Hitchens
Terwick Mill No. 11, Early Autumn
1945
oil on canvas, 20 × 41 in.
Bernard Jacobson Gallery

16 David Bomberg
Exmoor, Devon
1946
oil on canvas, 26 × 30 in.
Bernard Jacobson Gallery

17 Peter Lanyon
Landscape at Trevalgan
1951
oil on masonite, 48 × 45 in.
Bernard Jacobson Gallery

18 Edward Burra
Near Whitby, Yorkshire
1972
water-colour on paper,
31½ × 53½ in.
The Lefevre Gallery

19 William Tillyer
Urra
1992–93
acrylic on canvas with relief panel,
36 × 42 in.
Bernard Jacobson Gallery

20 Maurice Cockrill
Wheat Insemination
1992
oil on canvas, 32 × 39 in.
Bernard Jacobson Gallery

21 John Virtue
Landscape No. 178
1992
oil on canvas, 36 × 48 in.
Lisson Gallery

22 Wendy Connelly
Snowdonia: Early Spring
1993
oil, sand and pigment on board,
24 × 28 in.
Bernard Jacobson Gallery